Teaching the Taboo

Teaching the Taboo

COURAGE AND IMAGINATION IN THE CLASSROOM

Rick Ayers
William Ayers

Foreword by Haki R. Madhubuti

Teachers College, Columbia University
New York and London

Published by Teachers College Press, 1234 Amsterdam Avenue, New York, NY 10027

Library of Congress Cataloging-in-Publication Data

Ayers, Rick.
    Teaching the taboo : courage and imagination in the classroom / Rick Ayers, William Ayers. ; foreword by Haki R. Madhubuti.
        p. cm.
        Includes bibliographical references.
        ISBN 978-0-8077-5152-7 (pbk. : alk. paper)
        1. Effective teaching. 2. Teacher–student relationships. 3. Creative teaching. I. Ayers, William. II. Title.
    LB1025.3.A934 2011
    370.11'5–dc22   2010030295

ISBN 978-0-8077-5152-7

Printed on acid-free paper

Manufactured in the United States of America

18   17   16   15   14   13   12   11   8   7   6   5   4   3   2   1

Contents

FOREWORD

Knowledge, Kindness, Skills, and, Need I Say, Love

Teaching the Taboo: Courage and Imagination in the Classroom is a brave and necessary book. The authors, Rick and William Ayers, are brothers and seasoned educators who have dedicated themselves to studying, teaching, training, and engaging in social justice work worldwide, and especially in the underserved and under-appreciated communities. They have poured their years of deep investigation and participation in cultural and political struggle into these pages. In the tradition of Paulo Freire, Barbara A. Sizemore, A. S. Neill, and others, they take us on a journey seldom traveled and provide us with rich scholarship, fundamental deliberations on the meaning of service, cultural memory, and knowledge acquisition, all in the pursuit of excellence in teaching.

Most importantly, they are concerned–positively obsessed!–with the well-being of the nation's young people. Hanging deeply over their acute and well-placed observations is the failure of the 1954 *Brown v. Board of Education* ruling to right the disgraceful inequality in the nation's educational system. Both currently and historically, the "irreversible" harm of discrimination has reached beyond the Black community into the Latino, Native American, poor White, and Asian communities. Inadequate funding, poorly constructed curriculum, and unqualified, uncreative, and uninspired teachers represent the most visible aspects of the nation's education "problem." Deeply ingrained below the surface exists a stupefying ignorance of the many cultural forces directing and pulling students off-center: confrontations around power, sexuality, conflicting narratives, misunderstood cultural directives, White supremacy, gender realities, religious conflicts, and much more.

Any creative person who spends a day working or observing the activities in many public schools cannot fail to see disaster. According to the authors, these are not "spaces where happiness is cherished, reason is respected, integrity and dignity are upheld and revered, and authentic hope is viewed as a real possibility." Instead, we are slapped in the face with a narrative that highlights students as either victims and mindless robots or disadvantaged souls looking for solutions and success in an America that does not really exist for the majority of young people.

The Ayers brothers are about creating liberated zones locally and nationally. In this insightful study, they acknowledge that:

> Teachers are not invited to do missionary work, charity work, among the oppressed in our society. Instead, we have an opportunity to be in the presence of tremendous, powerful, insightful young people. We can join in the dance with students and provoke them with questions, challenges, tools, and reflection, but we are only useful agents in their educations if we replace charity with solidarity, patronizing with respect. This requires a leveling of power in the classroom and a concerted search for generative topics, resources, and questions to pursue together.

Today's challenge, especially in overcrowded, understaffed, and poorly funded urban schools, is to figure out how to reverse 50 years of a "go along to get along" mindset. In their inquiry, the Ayers brothers often use the tools of anthropology. When interacting with students, they incorporate, first and foremost, an atmosphere of respect, without making a priori negative assumptions. They then listen and respond in a nonthreatening, learned manner. As educators, the authors start from the recognition that "every human being, no matter who, is part miracle, part wonder, pulsing with the breath and beat of life, inhaling and exhaling, eating and hydrating, sweating and resting, prodded by sexual urges, evolved and evolving, shaped by genetics, twisted and gnarled and hammered by the unique experiences of living this or that singular life."

The struggle for truth starts at birth, when the master narrative finds comfort in lying to children, thereby nurturing and accommodating a "world" defined by fear, distrust, poverty, ignorance, politics, economics, and race, particularly as these are embedded in education and speech.

Why do millions of young people the world over become political and cultural activists primarily through fighting the state? As I. F. Stone often stated, all governments lie; and by extension presidents, teachers, mayors, police, generals, administrators, medical doctors, ministers, rabbis, and bankers all lie. We encourage a culture of liars, from our mass media to our most prized institutions. What a different education system we would have if the ideas of Adrienne Rich, Gwendolyn Brooks, and Toni Morrison were really discussed in high school literature. What if our high school civics and history courses included in the curriculum Noam Chomsky's writing on foreign affairs, Howard Zinn's accounting of America's wars, and Lerone Bennett Jr.'s report on Abraham Lincoln? Instead we get "top-tier liars" with no end in sight. The critical voices of Jonathan Kozol, Gloria Ladson-Billings, Carter G. Woodson, Barbara A. Sizemore, Edmund W. Gordon, and hundreds of others are left for the adventurous students to find on their own.

The common theme flowing throughout this taxing yet wonderful book is the authors' love of teaching, learning, and the act of engaged sharing at all levels of human activity. Such love promotes growth, intellectual development, and emotional maturation and leads students to an enlarged happiness, completely sold on their own unique possibilities. Part of the answer is encouraging an unlimited, yet pointed and searching, dialogue. This only works, of course, when all sides are heard and responded to respectfully with learned answers. Each side must understand that differences are human, cultural, and often gendered. We all have opinions, and hopefully we are looking for factors that will allow us to touch each other's hearts, hands, and minds.

The authors provide the example of Malik Dohrn, a wonderful 6th-grade math teacher from a junior high school in northern California who states, "There are two classes of folks in the current school debates: people who teach, like me, and people who talk about teaching." This was in reference to the current Secretary of Education and other administrators, researchers, and policy people. His point, with which I agree, is: If you are not directly on a daily basis in the game, strategy talk is theoretical and often beneficial only to suppliers and "turn-around" mercenaries who do not take into account the on-the-ground lives of individual children.

This is a book centered on young people and students. The authors make no quarter for bad teachers but see this blame game as a "straw man" that distracts us from the fundamental problem of the de-professionalism of the field where little respect for students or teachers exist:

> In the contested space of schools and education reform, the controlling metaphor posits education as a commodity rather than a right and a journey, and it imagines schools as little factories cranking out products, and teachers as glorified clerks or line employees, interchangeable functionaries whose job it is

to pass along the wisdom and the thinking of some expert, academic, or policy-maker: Here is the literary canon; here is the truth of history; here is the skill of reading. Education as a commodity reduces teaching to the simple and efficient delivery of the package called curriculum. There is little need for adjustment, no need for dialogue. The teacher is near the base of the education hierarchy, just above the student, who is the very bottom of the barrel.

I remember when teachers were expected to change the conversation, to jump-start imaginations, to question authority, and to right wrongs when it was within their province to do so. Fear permeates too many schools today. In most professions, ongoing advanced training is mandatory; advanced degrees are encouraged, paid for, and celebrated. In the best schools, teachers are involved in all aspects of their schools, from classroom management and curriculum updating to finance and fundraising. The best schools provide sports, music, theatre, travel, dance, smiles, friendly touches, math, chess, computer training, and book clubs. Art is not an afterthought but a destination of the mind. Nothing is off the table when it comes to our interaction with young minds, as long as it is healthy, reasoned, and in keeping with the best of modern pedagogy. All of this is enclosed in an environment of deep caring and love of students and the teaching profession. "Teaching the taboo" is actually teaching the truth unencumbered by the politics, economics, and ideology that dominates mass media and the lives of a low-information population. The authors state it best:

> Teaching the taboo is, in this sense, teaching the segregated and suppressed, the banned and the exiled. It's opening our eyes to the lively, dynamic moment before us. It's searching actively for something more. We are in pursuit of fulfillment, reaching for the rest of our humanity.

If given the chance, this book can be a defining text not only for those in the profession of education, but also for parents and lay readers nationwide who are truly concerned about our children and our future.

–Haki R. Madhubuti,
poet, founder and editor of Third World Press,
Ida B. Wells-Barnett University Professor at DePaul University

Prelude

Teaching, a transitive verb, an action word: the passing over or transmission of something from one person to another. The trouble starts right here with the suggestion of a "giver" and a "receiver." In reality, teaching–ubiquitous, dynamic, and abiding–expands into an entire universe: tutoring or guiding or mentoring, coaching and counseling, sharing, conversing, chattering, instructing, equipping, enlightening, freeing, informing, directing, encouraging, practicing, elaborating, preparing, back-and-forthing, stretching relentlessly toward the generous world of learning, teaching's twin: acquiring or attaining, studying and reading, wondering and wandering, plugging into and pushing through, initiating, building, creating, grinding, mastering, getting, practicing, elaborating, preparing, liberating. The two are intimately joined, one to the other, this primal human pursuit: We learn and from the instant we are born we also teach; we teach and we simultaneously learn to the last syllable of time.

Taboo, an often useful prohibition: Don't swim in still water; don't eat animals without an apology; don't marry your siblings. Here's more trouble: Western thought typically frames indigenous taboos as curious, ignorant, and superstitious, while conveniently shelving its own prohibitions, which themselves play a rigorous policing function, not always so useful, often maintaining in fact repressive, unjust, anti-democratic structures. Avoid certain neighborhoods at night! Always pass by hitchhikers! Don't talk to strangers! These injunctions are our own culturally bounded and socially constructed common wisdom, and there's more: Large numbers of poor families don't care about their children, or women in the Congo may grieve the loss of a child but it doesn't mean the same as the loss of a child here. These myths, too, are seen through our own everyday expectations, the fog of our own customs and assumptions.

The taboo is something beyond the formal or the legal—indeed, wherever we uncover the illicit or the forbidden, the unbridled or the unruly, anything that threatens to throw open the gates to tumultuous wild anarchy, here we'll likely find the taboo, greeting us with open arms and, we imagine, a lip-smacking leer. In U.S. culture, the taboo tends to fascinate itself with illicit sex, or it teeters on the edge of nuttiness obvious to the rest of us: Since Alex dumped him, dating has become a taboo topic with Shay. . . . Don't mention where Anita's dad got his money, it's a taboo in that household. . . . Hugging your students is, of course, strictly taboo.

Taboos lurk in every area of life, and schools are no exception: Lift the cover in any classroom, in any educational venue, and there they are, waiting. But precisely because taboos are so profoundly human, we each maintain the power of reinvention: We can question, re-inscribe, and repurpose many of the taboos we've inherited. Let in a single, dazzling beam of light, a bracing breath of air, and see what happens—you may find yourself advancing from the margins, sailing against the tide, speaking for the opposition. You may be—without even realizing it at first—teaching the taboo.

Introduction

Life is to be lived, not controlled; and humanity is won by continuing to play in the face of certain defeat. Our fate is to become one, and yet many—this is not prophecy, but description.

—Ralph Ellison, *Invisible Man*

We write this together as a reflection on two lifetimes of teaching, learning, rebelling, and wondering: These stories are from our classrooms, our communities, and our debates. *Teaching the Taboo* is meant as both provocation and invitation—a gesture of encouragement and inspiration for new and veteran teachers to pursue the deeper stuff, the better stuff that we all know is at the heart of successful teaching. The invitation is to look at the taken-for-granted in teaching, the everyday-ness of schools, the common sense of the entire educational project, and to open our eyes to a deeper reality through a pedagogy of questioning, by asking at every turn the most basic of questions: why? Why is education organized as an enterprise for the young? Why does formal education occur from kindergarten through 12th grade, or kindergarten through university? Why does there arrive a point in our lives when we act as if education is no longer needed? Why isn't any of this ever questioned?

Why the over-specialization of human activity, the alienation of the intellectual from the manual, for example, the head from the hand, the heart from the head, the creative from the functional? Why the disruption of any fluidity of function, and why no variation of work and capacity, no mobilization of intelligence and creativity and initiative and work in all directions at once?

1

Why, again, is there a hierarchy of teacher over student? Why does virtually every school have homework and grades and grade levels? Why is classroom management emphasized in teacher education? Why is attendance valued and enforced? Why is being on time important? Why indeed do we think of a productive and a service sector in our society, with education designated a service activity? Why is education separate from production? On and on, you get the picture: The key word as we trudge toward the hidden is *why*.

Our invitation is to live a teaching life of questioning, to imagine classrooms where every established and received bit of wisdom, common sense, orthodoxy, and dogma is open for examination, interrogation, and rethinking. The process of upending begins at the beginning: *why?* This simple word challenges every authoritarian impulse and every autocratic structure everywhere: *why?*

The provocation builds on that invitation: Can we construct our school and classroom practices on a base of fearless and relentless inquiry? For every confounding and repressive aspect of school as we find it, can we imagine something better? Can we see standing directly next to the situation as it is, the situation as it could be or should be? That is for us the point of first departure for teaching the taboo.

For example:

1. School is structured so resolutely around getting **right answers** that the problem of getting the right *questions*—and examining who gets to ask those questions and why, and who benefits from and gains power by framing and privileging certain questions and ignoring others—is left impenetrable and opaque. Subjects are taught in an atmosphere of punishment, declaring "gotcha" at every mistake. In place of this, imagine a school or a classroom where asking, framing, and pursuing their own questions becomes the central work of both teachers and students, where creativity and art are valued in an atmosphere that underscores mistakes as a pathway to deeper exploration.

2. School is built so stolidly on **summing up knowledge**, certifying and sanctioning all the stuff of the curriculum, that "reform" often amounts to little more than spreading the powerful arms of authorization into new realms (think: new standards for dance) or a more encompassing reach (think of the two dozen—and growing!—competencies to be mastered in 1st-grade language arts), and no one worries much about who established the curriculum or why.

In place of this, imagine a classroom where the question of what is worthwhile to know and experience is taken up as a living challenge to focus all student activity.

3. School has been so powerfully framed as a **commodity to be bought and sold** in the marketplace (just like a refrigerator or a stove), the system simply another business, identical in kind to Enron or Ford, that we begin to take the logic of layoffs and cutbacks as sensible managerial moves. Certification trumps the pursuit of knowledge, competition overwhelms learning. In place of this, imagine schools as expressions of participatory democracy, models of associative living, places powered by the notion that education is a human right and that the fullest development of all is the condition for the full development of each.

4. School so insistently treats the present moment as a kind of exalted **endpoint of history** (everything that ever happened brought us—rather miraculously, if you think about it—to this exact spot) that we lose sight of choices that demand to be made, as well as the obvious motion of change right in front of us. In place of this, imagine a classroom where all the themes, implicit and explicit, are built on a foundational idea that we are swirling through a living history, that nothing is guaranteed or foreordained, that we are, each and all of us, works-in-progress swimming shakily toward an uncertain and distant shore, and that what we do or don't do will have a major impact on where we land.

5. School so peremptorily assumes a **separation of itself from society** that we often miss the obvious sensory nature of life as it's lived in schools. In place of this, imagine a school or a classroom that tears down that wall and recognizes school and society as one and the same, and that acts out every day the belief that the classroom, far from being a preparation for life, is indeed life itself. Building community and trust and traditions and engagement are central lessons of a successful school.

There are more of course (and please add your own to this list), but these five barriers, five boundaries, five taboos, are at the front of our minds as we dive into the wreckage and organize ourselves to teach toward what could be, but is not yet. Can we imagine dramatically different schools? Can we find ways to breathe these classrooms to life in the real worlds we inhabit?

§

One of the odd things about organized education is that the standards, mile-posts, and markers of success are established almost exclusively by politicians and their sponsors in the world of big business—people whose claims to expertise are that they made it successfully through the old school system; they succeeded with the help and privileges from their families; they started a successful air-conditioning business or, most often, practiced law. Mining those barren experiences, they establish themselves as first fiddles in the school debates.

When educators fail to ask why that is so, and then push back, we abdicate responsibility to wonder openly and publicly about what an authentically educated person should look like, how an educated people should be characterized, or what knowledge and experiences we ought to value and teach in schools designed by and for a functioning democracy. We have too often settled instead for working hard and uncritically to meet markers of success set by the prodigies of politics and predatory economics.

Recently, a distinguished educator spoke to a rapt group of graduate students discussing work she was doing to help kids pass the New York Regents Exams—without a word about whether the exams are useful, intelligent, moral, or appropriate. This struck us as wrong: If legislators somewhere declared we should count the number of Jews in order to develop proper quotas, would we simply get to work to devise the best system? Of course not; we know better now. We would ask why, and then we would push back. But what of the exams? Shouldn't we here in our own house, ask the hard questions: Are they useful or good? Are they serving moral purposes? What are they for? Why?

If we never reflect about our roles and responsibilities, if we never ask normative questions about first purposes and fundamental principles, we will necessarily be complicit in some initiative or another that will likely offend our senses.

Schools, of course, serve the societies in which they're embedded in count-less direct and indirect ways—changing schools is no more a simple application of laws and procedures than is changing society. The schoolhouse is a mini-society, both an open window and an evident mirror into any given social order. If, for example, you'd have wanted insight into the workings of apart-heid in the old South Africa, you could simply have peeked into the schools. There you would have noticed White kids attending small classes with up-to-date equipment, and well-trained teachers dispensing a curriculum complicit with White supremacist assumptions; you'd have also seen Black kids in overcrowded, collapsing buildings being force-fed a steady diet of obedience and passivity. Clearly, one set of youngsters–the vast majority–was destined for the mines and the mills, the fields and the prisons, while the other set was being tutored to administer and profit from the intricate webs of injustice.

On and on, across time and place, the principle holds that each school attends its particular society: In any totalitarian society, schools are quite naturally built for obedience and conformity, and whatever else is taught, obedience is front-and-center, the hidden or open curriculum on every agenda; in a kingdom, schools teach fealty; in a racialized society, educational privileges and oppressions are distributed along the color line, and all lessons necessarily bend to xenophobia, illuminating everyone's place in the racial hierarchy. Education cannot be otherwise; schooling is never neutral.

Our schools, here and now, show us exactly who we are beneath whatever fear or anxiety, rhetoric or self-congratulatory platitudes we might embrace. Look closely: One of the first things we notice is a strict social hierarchy with youngsters attending separate and unequal schools based on income and class background. Some U.S. schools are funded to the tune of $30,000 or more per student per year, while other schools scrape by on a piddling fraction of that. Not surprisingly, given our peculiar history, schools are also segregated by ethnicity and race that overlap and interact in powerful ways with class: Schools for poor immigrant kids or the descendants of formerly enslaved people are walled off from schools available to the children of White people. Savage inequalities–a visible reality in Illinois and California and all across the country–are a defining characteristic of American schools.

Schools that claim to reflect "American values" also deny kids the right to speak, subject them to endless surveillance and unreasonable random searches; they insist that no one fight in school even as the school itself is militarized and turned into a base of war recruitment. Perhaps those are American values.

Our schools are increasingly on a wartime footing, havens for military mobilization and calls-to-arms, home to training programs where kids learn to wear uniforms, shoot guns, and march in step. Perhaps those are American values, too; after all, the United States maintains scores of military bases on foreign soil and spends a trillion dollars annually to stoke the war machine. Militarization extends as well into the culture of the school where police are a commonplace presence on high school campuses, and where obedience and conformity, the hallmarks of every authoritarian regime throughout history, are rewarded, while initiative, nonconformity, and free thinking are punished.

Schools tend to teach political indifference, emotional and intellectual dependency, and provisional self-esteem, one's proper place in the hierarchy of winners and losers, and the need to submit to certified authority. What, after all, are the lessons of report cards, grades, and the endless batteries of tests that play the part of autopsies rather than diagnostics? Don't trust yourself; seek approval from your betters. And what is the point of the established schedule and the set 50-minute periods, the uniform desks all in a row, the exhaustive use of time with no room to breathe and certainly no space to dream or wonder or wander or drift or reflect or imagine or just be bored? You are not important and unique; be malleable and productive only in terms established by a higher authority.

Our schools banish the unpopular, squirm in the presence of the unorthodox, hide the unpleasant. Much of what we call schooling forecloses or shuts down or walls off meaningful choice-making. There's little space for skepticism, irreverence, questioning, or doubt. While many of us long for teaching as something transcendent and powerful, too often we find ourselves locked in situations that reduce teaching to a kind of glorified clerking, passing along a curriculum of received wisdom and predigested and generally false bits of information.

All of these characteristics tell us more than we might want to know about the state of the United States at the dawn of the new millennium. If some of what we see is not as we would like it—aggressiveness, racial and class segregation, warlikeness, conformity, chauvinism—we can always search for justifications; we can retreat into mystification and our always-available, always precious and highly mannered good intentions.

Or we might choose a more hopeful option: We might conclude that some things *need* to be changed—we might even move toward joining hands with others, naming the world before us as in need of repair, and mobilizing ourselves as subjects in a living history and potential agents of transformation. We would be moving then, entering the deeply contested space of school and social change, without guarantees, but with an expanded sense of hope, confidence, and possibility. We would find ourselves in the land of the taboo.

§

Imagine arriving here from outer space on an investigative mission. Descending slowly toward the blue planet, you would notice that in large parts of the globe, people are getting up at the crack of dawn, working all day in fields or factories, living on low wages, and shipping a good deal of the items they produce to other parts of the globe. In these receiving parts, a main activity is consumption, and those not in the service industry tend to be dealing with information systems, abstractions, and networking. You might note that many people are apparently disposable as they are standing about aimlessly or locked up in cages.

In the producing parts of the globe, schooling is minimal or nonexistent, since getting kids into the work place early is a necessity: Work or die. But in the consuming places schooling goes on and on into adulthood. This division is blatant and clear and unjust, in spite of the 1948 standard toward education for all, expressed so eloquently in Article 26 of the United Nations Declaration of Human Rights: "Everyone has the right to education. Education shall be free, at least in the elementary and fundamental stages. Elementary education shall be compulsory. . . . Education shall be directed to the full development of the human personality and to the strengthening of respect for human rights and fundamental freedoms."

Today, the imperial dream of an unchallenged and grotesquely lopsided world is coming to a painful end. This is not the heralded "end of history," that weird ideology manufactured in the 1980s by the intellectual servants of power to explain and justify the imbalance and the injustice; rather, it is the end of the arrogant lust after a thousand-year *Pax Americana*. The evidence of terminal rot at the center is everywhere, and the accompanying collapse is all around us: an economic and financial emergency based on deep structural problems; an environmental crisis that cannot and will not be ignored; the demographic changes caused by globalization and immigration leading to the collapse of European-American majorities in the United States and Europe; the stalemate and impending defeat of Western military forces in Iraq, Afghanistan, and the entire region; and the various challenges to U.S. dominance from a number of directions, including North and South Asia, Latin America, a tenuously united Europe, and oddly jerry-rigged entities such as the BRIC alliance (Brazil, Russia, India, China).

This historic moment could surely be violent and horrifying, or it could be—why not?—beautiful and filled with new hope and possibilities. That is in part up to us: It depends on how we think and how we act. In education, this new reality challenges us to reconsider every assumption and to reexamine first and fundamental principles.

We note and face this altered landscape and these dynamic real-world conditions at the dawn of a new millennium as an essential first step toward re-imagining the project of schooling—teaching and learning, curriculum and instruction—in radically new ways.

For the most part, education in the advanced centers is set up to maintain things as they are—focusing on training soldiers and prison guards, a great army of the unemployed, as well as operators for the "new economy" with skills in cyber-technology, management, and domination, urging students to study hard to "stay competitive"—that is, to beat and dominate other societies. As the crisis sets in and the party is almost over, we can choose to stick our heads in the sand, or we might rethink our relationships with one another and with the rest of the world. We might note that we never enlisted in this economic war against the rest of the world. We may, with our students, imagine new ways of thinking and being. And this will lead us to new ways of defining an educated person, of imagining—together with our students—a new world with new social relations, with new skills and passions and dreams.

The end of empire challenges us to stop fidgeting with the micro-data and start envisioning a whole new world with new approaches to production and consumption and participation, as well as wildly new relationships with one another and spanking new educational possibilities. It suggests a pedagogy of equity and engagement, one that is driven by and serves the needs of the rising majority, the currently marginalized communities, and the victims of empire. It insists that we notice, construct, or revive models of liberatory education, that we reject and resist the top-down, irrelevant, straitjacket schools we have, and strike for an alternative: participatory democracy, problem-posing and humanizing curriculum, student- and community- and family-led schools, classrooms without walls conducted in the streets and parks and workplaces and playgrounds—all of these ache to be invented and initiated, not in Washington policy parlors but on the ground, from the bottom, in the communities.

§

With our eyes open, we cannot now easily or even sensibly accede to a regime of test and punish, certainly not the widely discredited "No Child Left Behind" initiative, nor the rebranded but essentially identical "Race to the Top" program. The underpinnings of each of these campaigns is the explicit charge to American kids to "be competitive," to outperform and hence to enlist in the effort to dominate rising populations of China, India, and elsewhere. Nothing about the full development of human potential, nor about justice, joy, or peace—it's all business, and the business is not good. Why should anyone sign up for such an economic competition? When were all American teachers drafted as soldiers in *that* war?

The "achievement gap," the shameful distance between students that fractures along lines of race and class, is a leading weapon in the competition-war; it stands in our national debates as an unfathomable mystery that simply can't be cracked, or the focus of anxiety and remediation and, of course, more research. Politicians are shocked, *shocked* that the gap can't be overcome, while many thousands of academics and researchers enlist in a kind of jobs-program, continually circling around it, probing and scratching their heads.

But the achievement gap is nothing more than a carefully constructed mechanism of power and it simply cannot be abolished in its own terms because standardized testing is calibrated precisely to reflect students' class experience and social capital. This still holds: The best predictor of how a student will do on any high school standardized tests is how she did in her first test in 3rd grade. And the best predictor of how she will do on that first test is her parents' income. A lot of time, effort, money, and nonsense could be avoided if we simply lined kids up by class background and sorted them out. It would have the added benefit of being honest.

Testing in America is not only culturally biased in obvious ways, but it's a self-perpetuating validation machine designed so that those with more social capital and privilege will land on the top of the pile. Here's one example: Every year, the College Board runs "test questions" on its standardized tests. If the test-takers they've identified as "good students" do badly on a question, and if those who have been identified as weak students get the same question right, it's thrown out. The College Board doesn't even have to understand why the test worked this way. The tautological thinking guarantees reproduction of the same results year after year. No amount of heroic volunteer test-prep classes run after school in urban centers will change that reality.

The same self-reproducing processes are in place in terms of grades. Curriculum is structured to exclude student knowledge and capacity; teaching is promoted by the powerful only when it appears as disembodied instruction calibrated for the discourse practices of White middle-class children; courses proceed under a punishment regime, dunning students for mistakes and failures every step of the way; the arts are suspect and marginalized, as they represent independent thinking and a disruption of power; and community projects that engage students are banned.

As education is increasingly framed as a commodity purchased in the marketplace rather than a public good and a human right, it is reduced to a Social Darwinist model of competition, sorting, and external criteria for success, and it's desperately enacted in classrooms across the country. We are told repeatedly that we benefit from the greatest democracy and the greatest amount of freedom that makes us the envy of the world, while in our schools we see the iron hand of authoritarianism—more intrusive, more demanding, more concerned with the tiniest details of education. Teachers, families, and children should not accept this. We can and must build, from the bottom, a new 21st-century education that is vital and engaged, responsive to the needs of humanity, and geared to the challenges of now.

We can see, if we choose, that the emperor has no clothes and that everywhere there is a new blossoming of culture and political action. And, yes, even thoughtful, reconsidered schooling is rising before us. We cannot sensibly wait around for the federal government to lead a revolution in education: *It's never going to happen.* It's up to us, teachers and students and communities, to get extra-busy, and to unleash thunder and power from the bottom. Our task, really, is to get on board with these creative outbursts of change, or be left by the side of the road, forever writing the algorithms and rules on the chalk blackboard even as the students have charged out the classroom door on a mission of re-invention and repair. We must embrace the taboos of today to give birth to the dreams of tomorrow.

§

In a school focused on the needs and dreams of the broad, even global community, we would be inspired by fundamental principles of democracy, including a common faith in the incalculable value of every human being. In education we would recognize that the full development of each is the condition for the fullest development of all, and conversely that the fullest development of all is the condition for the full development of each. One implication of this principle is that in a truly democratic spirit, whatever the wisest and most privileged parents want for their kids, that is exactly what we as a community want for all of our children. A vibrant democracy would place at the center the broader concerns of society, the needs of the individual in balance with the collective good, the common interest, and the many intersections of interest.

Faith in the value of each human being, this embrace of a common humanity, has huge implications for educational policy: Racial privilege is wrong, class separation unjust, disparate funding immoral. There is simply no justification in a democracy for the existence of one school for wealthy White kids funded generously, and another school for the children of formerly enslaved people funded meagerly. That reality offends the very idea that each person is equal in value and regard, and reflects instead the reactionary idea that some of us are more deserving and more valuable than others.

The democratic injunction has big implications for curriculum and teaching as well, for what is taught and how. We want students to be able to think for themselves, to make judgments based on evidence and argument, to develop minds of their own. We want them to ask fundamental questions—who in the world am I? How did I get here and where am I going? What in the world are my choices? How in the world shall I proceed?—and to pursue the answers wherever they might take them. In a democracy we refuse obedience and conformity in favor of initiative, courage, imagination, creativity, and more. These qualities cannot be delivered in top-down ways, but must be modeled and nourished, encouraged and defended.

While our profession is suffering insult and contempt from the talking heads of media and policy, there is a secret that all good teachers know. We know that this is the most delightful, meaningful, and important profession. The most important things we do—being with young people through crucial moments in their growth, modeling ethical caring, and unleashing curiosity and imagination—are never measured by quantitative metrics. But these are the reasons we keep coming back, starting each day anew.

The best teaching encourages students to develop the capacity to name the world for themselves, to identify the obstacles to their full humanity, and the courage to act upon whatever the known demands. This kind of education is characteristically eye-popping and mind-blowing—always about opening doors and opening minds as students forge their own pathways into a wider, shared world.

In an educational project that values democracy, teachers would devote as much attention to the creation of community as to the "material" to be read and studied together. Students would learn the value of the routines of the community as well as how to exercise agency and initiative within it. We would pay particular attention to the learning environment—for there can be authoritarian as well as democratic spaces. Do the students help create it? Is it malleable and inviting? Can it take us new places? Is power recognized as each contributes to the whole?

Not only do we have to think about the classroom, the hallways, the outside, but we also need to make the broader community—public transportation, theaters, sewage plants, urban gardens, everything—part of the learning environment. We need to pay attention to our relationship with colleagues—can we collaborate, commiserate, and conspire together? Students have a right to understand the purposes in the educational project and to help create that purpose, to be included. Schools are built around not just tasks and tests but around community-generated rituals and traditions, some of which begin as single events but become, at students' insistence, regular practices. School is the site of rites of passage, which can be either cruel and stultifying or creative and expansive, depending on the kind of work we do.

§

Can we imagine that another world—a more humane and peaceful place, a more harmonious and balanced experience—is not only desirable but possible? As the Brazilian teacher-organizer Paolo Freire pointed out, "From the very first day of class, (teachers) must demonstrate to students the importance of imagination for life. Imagination helps curiosity and inventiveness, just as it enhances adventure, without which we cannot create" (Freire 1998, p. 51). Can we imagine schools where the art of meaningful reading is the norm, the development of the disposition of the artist a common goal? Can we name the obstacles to creating that world, link up with one another as we trudge forward and work toward building something entirely new under the sun?

If society cannot be changed under any circumstances, if there is nothing to be done, not even small and humble gestures toward something better, well, that ends the conversation. Our sense of agency shrinks and our choices collapse. What more is there to say? We are diminished immeasurably, our sense of purpose and morality reduced to the plane of a desperate fight in the swamp for basic survival. Our humanity is erased. But if a fairer, saner, and more just social order is both desirable and possible—that is, if some of us can join one another to imagine and build a participatory movement for justice, a public space for the enactment of democratic dreams—our field opens slightly.

There would still be much to be done, for nothing would be entirely settled. We would still need to find ways to stir ourselves from passivity, cynicism, and despair; to reach beyond the superficial barriers that wall us off from one another; to resist the flattening effects of consumerism and the blinding, mystifying power of the familiar social evils—White supremacy, patriarchy, and homophobia, for example; to shake off the anesthetizing impact of much official claptrap and the authoritative voices that dominate our schools and universities, the airwaves and the media; and to revitalize our imaginations and act on behalf of what the known demands, linking our conduct firmly to our consciousness. We would be moving, then, with purpose and a measure of hope.

Nothing is settled, surely, once and for all, but a different order of question presents itself: Who should be included? What do we owe one another? What is fair and unfair? And always, the enduring questions in education: Education for what? Education for whom? Education toward what kind of social order?

§

All teaching is enacted in a specific here and now, all of it brought to life in the mud and muck of the world as we find it—this prairie or that field, this street or that other one. We don't choose the world as such; rather, we are thrust into a world that is already there, up and running. We race to catch up, taking the world as it is to start, unvarnished, and plunging forward as participants toward the new and the unknown. If we are to live fully, deeply, purposefully— if we are to experience both the beauty and the pain of it, if we are to add our little weight to the balance—we need to open our eyes and get busy.

Opening our eyes is not as simple as it might sound. Often, we kid ourselves that all history is past, and that we are somehow *not* moving inside a living, constantly constructed history; we act as if all the "historic moments" happened before we got here. And, no doubt, we delude ourselves that, had any of us been around for the abolition struggle, say, women's suffrage, or the fight for the 8-hour day, not only would we have been on the side of the angels, but we'd have been gutsy and agitating heroes. This is not only a distorted view of history, but, more important, it blinds us to the present, to all the inherent dangers and all the yeasty possibilities that are before us right here, right now. When we experience this moment as somehow a point of arrival, the only possible outcome, we are rendered powerless to imagine another world, or to act on behalf of what could be, but is not yet. We get it wrong about then, but worse, we get it wrong about now.

In reality, during the days of slavery, most White Americans took it as normal and unchangeable—just the natural order of things. It took acts of imagination and courage and focused effort to break with common sense and the taken-for-granted. A few did, in defiance of their government, the law, their church, and their parents. And then more broke with the everyday taken-for-granted, and eventually the idea of slavery as a normal, natural state was undermined and overcome. And, of course, we're all abolitionists now, and we flatter ourselves to think that we'd all have been abolitionists when it mattered.

And so today—what are the injustices and imbalances, the unnecessary sufferings, the pain and the harm that we simply cannot see? Fifty years from now, what glaring atrocity of today will we recognize as totally unacceptable?

History is always in-the-making, and we are—each one of us—works-in-progress; what we do or fail to do will inevitably make a difference. Nothing is predetermined, and we are acting largely in the dark with our limited consciousness and our contingent capacities. This can be cause for despair if your mood is solemn, but it can, as well, open to a field of possibility. It can call on us to get busy.

As Nina Simone challenged us: Why don't you see it? Why don't you feel it? I don't know. I don't know.

We're reminded that privilege is always anesthetizing, and that the privileged are necessarily blind to their own blind spots. It's of course an effort for White people to see the obstacles placed in the paths of people of color, for men to see the routine injuries visited upon women, for the able-bodied to feel the dislocation and banal discrimination experienced by so many. And so it is for straight people: We have to stretch to see the pain of children routinely beaten and taunted and marginalized in our schools, of teachers asked to deny their identities, of parents pushed around in unfriendly settings, of human beings asked to deny their closest loved ones.

As teachers are increasingly de-skilled and hammered into interchangeable cogs in a large unthinking and unfeeling bureaucracy, as pressure builds to reduce teaching to a set of manageable and easily superviseable tasks and to sum it up on the basis of a single simple-minded metric, to strip it of any moral purpose or intellectual engagement or creative action whatsoever, it becomes ever more important to find ways to resist, to fight back, to rescue teaching from the forces of mindlessness and carelessness.

Teachers of the taboo are engaged outsiders. We build an identity in part as exiles—restless, in motion, unsettled and unsettling, people who do not feel entirely at home in our homes—and in part as exuberant, passionate, committed people, filled with delight as well as grief and anger. We want to live willfully, gratified if uncomfortable disrupters of the status quo, advocates of decency and justice, critics of orthodoxy and dogma, stereotype and received wisdom of every kind, all the reductive categories that limit thought and communication.

But we are also inside the schools, for better or for worse. We might try to see our individual and collective positions in this way—as both insiders and outsiders we become more vital participants in the fullness of life, and simultaneously removed from and slightly tangent to every one of our associations. We cultivate, then, a state of steady alertness and a spirit of opposition rather than accommodation, of dissent against the status quo at a time when the struggle on behalf of the marginalized and the disadvantaged is so unfairly weighted. Our ideal is knowledge, enlightenment, and truth on the one hand, and on the other, human freedom, emancipation, liberation for all, with emphasis on the dispossessed. Our task is to see the world as fully as we can, and to speak up and speak out on behalf of the truth as we understand and experience it.

It is in this sense that teaching is an intellectual and ethical enterprise. It requires thoughtful and caring people to carry it forward—not a head without a heart, and not a sweetie pie without a brain. Teachers need to both think and feel their way into what they're doing. It's at the intersection of the intellectual and the ethical where teachers find their bearings. It's here that we crawl toward love—not love as a "throbbing heart or a soulful imploring" as Pat Carini has written, but love as a call to action, an impulse that insists that all human beings matter, even when law or custom or social practice or restriction says otherwise.[1] Ours becomes a stance of solidarity, not charity.

§

The prophetic poet Audre Lorde wrote: "When we speak we are afraid our words will not be heard nor welcomed. But when we are silent we are still afraid."[2] It is better, then, to speak out, and to act up. Since all life is a risk, stepping forward affords at least the hope of something better. It is in this spirit of resistance and hope that we go in search of a pedagogy of the possible—teaching the taboo.

ONE.

Emancipate Yourselves from Mental Slavery

Real education means to inspire people to live more abundantly, to learn to begin with life as they find it and make it better, but the instruction so far given Negroes [and still today] in colleges and universities [and elementary and secondary schools] has worked to the contrary.

—Carter G. Woodson, *The Mis-Education of the Negro*

Paulo Freire, whose work formed the basis for many successful literacy campaigns worldwide and became one of the best-known practitioners and theorists of teaching toward freedom, was an inspiration to Third World liberation struggles throughout Latin America and Africa. But the ideas that shaped his efforts did not simply spring fully formed from his mind. They were a result of the revolutionary period he inhabited and the range of wildly robust social movements on the ground.

Howard University student Charles Cobb,[3] along with Ella Baker of the Student Non-Violent Coordinating Committee (SNCC), [4] without knowing Freire's work, articulated an approach that corresponded in powerful ways with his vision. In the American South and throughout the global south, organizers recognized that wisdom and leadership resided in the experiences and practices of the poorest and most marginalized people in society. Instead of imposing a top-down, information transmission model, radical educators insisted that curriculum should be co-constructed by students acting in their own interests.

At the same time, and in response to the growth of the national liberation movements against colonial domination, an explosion of liberationist intellectual re-evaluations reverberated throughout society. This was reflected in a critique of traditional, supposedly objective journalism (by New Journalists such as Studs Terkel, Joan Didion, and Hunter S. Thompson); a challenge to the master narrative in history (by writers such as Howard Zinn, Adam Hochschild, and Eric Foner); a rethinking of the Western canon and colonialist mentality in literature (by critics such as Roberto Retamar and Edward Said); a questioning of the great man theory of science (by Thomas Kuhn); and a reclaiming of indigenous sensibilities in poetry and literature (by poets such as Pablo Neruda, Gwendolyn Brooks, and Amiri Baraka, and novelists such as Gabriel Garcia Marquez, Ngugi wa Thiong'o, and Toni Morrison).

In 1963, Charlie Cobb wrote a brief proposal for Freedom Schools in the SNCC organizing work in Mississippi. He explained that, while the Black children in the South were denied many things—decent school facilities, honest and forward-looking curriculum, fully qualified teachers—the fundamental injury was "a complete absence of academic freedom and students are forced to live in an environment that is geared to squashing intellectual curiosity and different thinking."[5] He described the classrooms of Mississippi as "intellectual wastelands," and he challenged himself and others "to fill an intellectual and creative vacuum in the lives of young Negro Mississippi, and to get them to articulate their own desires, demands and questions." Their own desires, their own demands, their own questions—for African Americans living in semi-feudal bondage, managed and contained through a system of law and custom as well as outright terror, this was beyond imagination.

> The aim of the Freedom School curriculum will be to challenge the student's curiosity about the world, introduce him to his particularly "Negro" cultural background, and teach him basic literacy skills in one integrated program. That is, the students will study problem areas in their world, such as the administration of justice, or the relation between state and federal authority. Each problem area will be built around a specific episode which is close to the experience of the students.

Student experience and student insight was a driving force in classroom matters, and Freire, Cobb, and others approached education as a kind of community organizing, community empowerment, and not simply the transmission of static knowledge from above. The thread of this approach has been included more recently in the work of SNCC veteran Bob Moses in the Algebra Project. Others who elaborated these and similar liberationist views included A. S. Neill, Gloria Ladson-Billings, Asa Hilliard, W.E.B. DuBois, Carter G. Woodson, Septima Clark, Fanny Coppin, Sylvia Ashton-Warner, Carol Lee, Herb Kohl, Maxine Greene, and many more.

We look to the Freedom Schools of 1964 without a hint of nostalgia—we have no longing for a ship that's already left the shore. They happened; they were powerful but short-lived; they left a slightly abraded surface. We recognize, too, that looking backward ought to always come with a red-letter warning: The concrete conditions and circumstances have changed; we are now required to make our own contributions in our own time and place; the pathway, the content, and the curriculum must be of, by, and for this moment and this community. We might, then, take inspiration and attitude, sustenance and stance, from the Mississippi experience as starting point only, as an orientation toward launch. And we might imagine and perhaps bring to life something utterly new. We will have to teach the taboo, if we choose to do so, in the here and now. And in the here and now, as in the 1960s, the great work will be done in the barrios and ghettos, the villages and forgotten corners, by people on the ground, in the communities. This is where we must turn to find hope and inspiration, not to the policy-makers or the secretaries of education. Like the new journalists, we must stop being palace-watchers and turn our attention to the people, to communities, in order to find transformative education as it is practiced today.

John Dewey pointed out the many ways that schooling evolves to accommodate and serve the social order of the day. If early American schools were to teach children basic literacy for social interaction (one-room schoolhouse), 19th-century schooling evolved to serve an industrial order with organizational efficiency and skill-building (factory-model school); the 20th century saw an explosion of higher education as the U.S. economy assumed the position of controlling the levers of a global economy. Schooling today is at a crossroads: Will it simply serve an old order that has reached the stage of crisis? Will it fight for a future in which a new economic bubble has been inflated and Americans get back on the saddle of world domination? Or can we—will we—fashion schools that allow students to envision a new relationship with people of the world, a new purpose for social production besides the creation of more commodities? Educational visionaries do not simply slot children into narrow roles determined by those in power; they help children and society reinvent our lives, generating structures that reflect our deepest values.

It's up to us. Charlie Cobb explains that one of the things holding back the Freedom Movement in the south was African American people themselves accepting definitions of their own inferiority. When SNCC organizers and the community itself refused those caricatures through action, people rose up, not only to take up the struggle, but also to transform themselves in the process to be worthy of the challenges that faced them:

> Most of us organizing soon learned that our main challenge was getting Black people to challenge themselves. Stated another way, people would have to redefine themselves. That was the foundation on which White supremacy could be effectively challenged. As SNCC organizer Larry Guyot, a native Mississippian, put it once: "To battle institutions, we must change ourselves first."[6]

§

Teachers go into teaching because of a deep concern for young people, a desire to change the world for the better, or a hope to share some part of the world with the young. To accomplish even the most modest goals on the side of our students, we soon discover that we must be bold and take risks.

If teachers choose a life of risk-taking, their troubles begin: How do you introduce important issues without being just another authoritarian presence in your students' lives? How do you avoid trampling on their insights, points of views, and experiences?

Charlie Cobb and Ella Baker's indictment of Mississippi's schools half a century ago can be applied verbatim and with chilling accuracy to contemporary schools in New York or Chicago or Los Angeles, and most places in between: "a complete absence of academic freedom," "an environment that is geared to squashing intellectual curiosity." Although generally accurate, this miserable description finds its truest application in schools that house large numbers of poor, Native, Latino, and African American youngsters. Here, children and youth encounter something that looks and smells and walks and talks exactly like an antiquated and brutish colonial system: a school experience designed to pacify and domesticate, to promote and police the existing hierarchies of privilege and oppression in which poor youngsters know their place (the street corner, the charity line, the prison) and accept it with a minimum of bitterness and with zero resistance. After all, the authoritative voices repeat in icy chorus, whatever structural obstacles might have once existed—segregation, say, institutionalized hierarchies built on color and caste and class—were happily swept away long ago and we are, all of us, free at last. What do you believe? Your own unreliable eyes, or the categorical and commanding account of the experts—majestic, triumphant, settled.

Further, "Your reading levels and test scores don't lie"—you earned your failure, now own it. For students to question the circumstances of their lives is unacceptable; to persist is to become resistant, and then recalcitrant. Either way—compliance or rebellion—the humanity of these students lies precariously in the balance.

Education at its best is habit-breaking and reorienting—it's about opening doors, opening minds, inviting students to become more capable and powerful actors and choice-makers as they forge their own pathways into a wider world. Education at its best is the practice of freedom. But much of what we call schooling—so evident in schools for the poor—forecloses or shuts down or walls off meaningful choice-making. While many of us may long for teaching as something transcendent and powerful, we find ourselves too often locked in situations that reduce teaching to a kind of glorified clerking. A fundamental choice and challenge for teachers, then, is this: to acquiesce to the machinery of control, or to take a stand with our students in a search for meaning and a journey of transformation; to be a prison guard or an educator; to teach obedience and conformity, or to teach its polar opposite: initiative and imagination, the capacity to name the world, to identify the obstacles to your full humanity, and the courage to act upon whatever the known demands—to teach the taboo.

§

Let's look for a moment at schools as they actually are—all the common-sense assumptions, the broad commonplace features and activities, the reality beyond the rhetoric. What is expected of us, teachers and students, parents and administrators? What have we become accustomed to? The simplest, most eloquent answers typically come from the mouths of students themselves. Whenever James Herndon asked his kids why they were bowing down to some arbitrary or particularly maddening and inane school custom, their response was inevitably because that's "the way it spozed to be."[7]

The way it spozed to be is characterized by division and isolation—students against teacher, teachers against the administration, the union versus the board. Worse, school divides students against one another, each on his or her own, through mechanisms of grades and tests and rankings, and it further divides and alienates students within themselves, all the arbitrary demarcation of experience and knowledge into disciplines and subjects, the disconnection of interest and relevance, initiative and courage from school-sanctioned success. And those grades and scores: a reductive shorthand that turns kids into stickfigures, lifeless and brittle, and trumpets the triumph and unambiguous wonder of objectivity, when in fact objectification itself is their greatest problem and weakness. All this disunity and disengagement, all the segregation and isolation—where does it leave us?

The way it spozed to be bows before numbers, genuflects to quantification, and values anything that can be counted over everything that can't. Schools promote a flattened world where things get counted, or, as one notable education scholar and professor told us, everything that exists, exists in some amount, and so everything must be measurable. We asked him about love, hope, beauty, joy, imagination, and possibility, and he said we were being foolish. The "measure of man" is the impossible ideal, the mis-measure of humanity the inevitable outcome.

We're always a little astonished when reformers come forward with schemes to "integrate the curriculum" or to "create real-world projects and internships." Why was the curriculum segregated in the first place? When did the unreal world get such a mighty foothold? Why does the student feel walled off from society and the Earth anyway?

If we peek for a moment beneath the official high-sounding justification for compulsory schooling—to create good and productive citizens, say, or to allow students to reach their full potential, to unlock the talent and energy of each—there's a truth that dares not speak its name: The way it spozed to be is designed to mold and control the herd, to engineer and shape up the unruly crowd, to grind potentially free people into obedient soldiers, servile and efficient laborers, mindless consumers. Our rulers were not always so coded, so reluctant to say it plainly. In 1909, Woodrow Wilson said, "We want one class of persons to have a liberal education, and we want another class of persons, a very much larger class of necessity in every society, to forgo the privilege of a liberal education and fit themselves to perform specific difficult manual tasks."[8]

The way it spozed to be is designed to sort youngsters into these classes, to find for each a proper role in the existing social order. Schools reward conformity and mindless habits of obedience for a reason, and they relentlessly punish deviance with a purpose.

If you envision the whole enterprise as a vast pyramid, with the elite perched upon the groaning masses at the base, entire schools and whole districts will produce all winners, and others mostly losers. It's true: Jonathon Kozol has written brilliantly about the "savage inequalities" that result in two high schools, for example, separated by a few miles, one of which has a beautiful campus and a modern building, teachers with advanced degrees and a deep commitment to teaching these students, and a budget that allows them to spend an average of $20,000 per student, per year. [9] The other has less than $5,000 to spend on each student, and kids attend overcrowded classes in a dilapidated building. The message is lost on no one.

It goes beyond this. Marty Haberman describes a "pedagogy of poverty" that practically guarantees failure for students stepping into a larger world. [10] The teaching acts that constitute this pervasive pedagogy of poverty are these: "giving information, asking questions, giving directions, making assignments, monitoring seatwork, reviewing assignments, giving tests, reviewing tests, assigning homework, reviewing homework, settling disputes, punishing noncompliance, marking papers, and giving grades."

There are other teacher responsibilities—staff meetings, parent conferences, and record-keeping—but this basic menu of teaching practices constitutes a common experience and expectation. Undergirding this practice, in Haberman's view, are four principles:

1. Teaching is what teachers do. Learning is what students do. Therefore, students and teachers are engaged in different activities.
2. Teachers are in charge and responsible. Students are those who still need to develop appropriate behavior. Therefore, when students follow teachers' directions, appropriate behavior is being taught and learned.
3. Students represent a wide range of individual differences. Many students have handicapping conditions and lead debilitating home lives. Therefore, ranking of some sort is inevitable; some students will end up at the bottom of the class while others will finish at the top.
4. Basic skills are a prerequisite for learning and living. Students are not necessarily interested in basic skills. Therefore, directive pedagogy must be used to ensure that youngsters are compelled to learn their basic skills.

Of course, this pedagogy fails to educate kids, fails to engage their minds or their energies, and succeeds only in creating resentment and burnout everywhere. A pattern of behaviors and beliefs ensues that Haberman calls the "ideology of non-work": Each day, and every bit of work, is disconnected from anything that preceded or will follow it; a willingness on the part of teachers to demand little beyond showing up—and to accept virtually any excuse for lateness or absence as long as kids aren't too disruptive; relationships that are authoritarian and nonmutual. All of it adds up to a pervasive sense of passivity, cynicism, purposelessness, fatalism, and despair.

It doesn't have to be that way, of course, but that's the way it is. Haberman notes: "The pedagogy of poverty requires that teachers who begin their careers intending to be helpers, models, guides, stimulators, and caring sources of encouragement transform themselves into directive authoritarians in order to function in urban schools." We can't imagine a 10-year-old (or a college undergraduate) telling friends, "I've decided to grow up to become a teacher because I can't wait to discipline the little miscreants," or "I've decided to teach so that I can sort out the winners from the losers." Haberman notes that "the gap between expectations and reality means that there is a pervasive, fundamental irreconcilable difference between the motivation of those who select themselves to become teachers and the demands of urban teaching."

He offers an interesting and helpful guide for teachers who might have the courage to begin to construct an alternative. He argues that good teaching is more likely going on, for example, whenever students are:

- involved with issues they regard as vital concerns
- being helped to see major concepts, big ideas, and general principles
- planning what they will be doing
- applying ideals such as fairness, equity, or justice to their world
- actively involved
- asked to think about an idea in a way that questions common sense
- redoing, polishing, or perfecting their work
- reflecting on their own lives and how they have come to believe and feel as they do

In other words—and this seems so plainly obvious—all kids need opportunities to create and to build, to invent and compose, to follow their interests to their furthest limits, to be imaginative, curious, and venturesome. They need to be themselves—uniquely, flexibly, autonomously, integrally—and they need to be part of something beyond themselves. All of this is more likely and more possible if they're in the company of grownups, of teachers perhaps, who are themselves curious and adventurous, thoughtful, caring, competent, and balanced. This is what we might aspire to.

Granted, we've drawn this portrait of schools as they are, of the way it spozed to be, overbroadly; granted, too, our perceptions and judgments of school are various, and school cannot possibly be painted as a single experience, the same for all. All true, but is this picture impossibly opaque, impenetrable, incomprehensible? You decide, but for anyone who has spent any time in an American school, it's got a ring of recognizable authenticity.

§

Lots of schools built for the industrial age look like little factories, and the metaphor of production dominates the discourse–assembly lines, management and supervision, quality control, productivity, and outputs. Students are intermittently the raw materials moving dumbly down the assembly line while value is added by the workers/teachers, or the workers themselves, workers-in-training, of course.

Reflecting the current paradigm of neoliberal market-driven business models, schools have become sites of endless competition, between students, between school sites, between teachers, and between communities. In a self-fulfilling prophecy, the school czars have created a Hobbesian nightmare, a "war of all against all." And the stakes in this Social Darwinist game are high–the difference between affluence and life on the streets.

When a school drops a further metaphoric notch, it functions as a prison, and an increasing number of schools do. Students become its little political prisoners–the most wide-awake of them know it. Compelled by the state to attend, handed a schedule, a uniform, and a rulebook, sent to a specific designated space of cell blocks, monitored constantly and controlled relentlessly–Pledge of Allegiance: 9:00; No talking; Bathroom break: 10:15–10:20; No eating in the classroom; Lunch: 11:45–12:05; Boys and girls form separate lines; Dismissal bell: 3:10; No running in the hallways; on and on and on, the whole catalog of coercion under forced confinement–every young body the object of domination and control.

The "Uniform Discipline Code" of the Chicago Public Schools, a case in point, grows, it seems, an inch a year. Its putative goal is "To promote desirable student conduct and behavior," its approach to "Codify the penalties that shall be applicable system-wide, yet retain administrative flexibility in their application"—a task that could keep a battery of lawyers busy for months, with a neat loophole large enough for a yellow school bus full of adolescents to drive through.

The book has preliminary chapters on student responsibilities and rights, and then onto parents, teachers, and principals—each group divided between rights and responsibilities. Students and teachers are instructed, for example, to "Observe basic standards of cleanliness, modesty, and good grooming," while principals, interestingly, have no comparable responsibility according to the book. Perhaps it's assumed that principals, but not teachers, already know how to dress. Student responsibilities go on and on: "Be honest and courteous," "Have pride in your school," "Improve your performance upon notice of unsatisfactory progress"—21 bullet points in all. Parents have only 12 points, the first of which speaks volumes about expectations: "Present to school officials your case/cause in a calm, reasoned manner." One can feel the gulf, the wall, the antagonism. Teachers are, of course, to "Devote school hours exclusively to official duties"—is this really needed?—and principals to "Notify the Chicago Police Department as necessary." Really.

"Student Misconduct" is divided into six neat groupings: Group 1 is "*inappropriate* student behaviors" such as "Running and/or making excessive noise in the hall or building," or "Being improperly dressed," all of which result in conferences. Group 2 is *disruptive*, Group 3 *seriously disruptive*, Group 4 *very seriously disruptive*, and Group 5 *most seriously disruptive behavior*, each with its accompanying and escalating sanctions and punishments. Group 6 consists of "Acts of misconduct [that] include illegal student behaviors that not only *most seriously disrupt* the orderly educational process . . . but also mandate . . . disciplinary action" from 10-day suspensions to expulsions.

Group 2 behaviors include "Posting or distributing unauthorized or other written materials on school grounds"; Group 3 "Gambling" and "Forgery"; Group 4, "Extortion," "Assault," and "Disorderly Conduct"; Group 5, "Aggravated assault," "Gang activity, including repeated overt displays of gang affiliation." Group 6 acts include things such as "Arson," "Bomb threats," "Murder," "Kidnapping," and "Sex violations." Kidnapping? Murder?

Whew!

The book ends with a convenient six-page Glossary written by an idiot savant with a law degree: "Indecent proposition—An unsolicited sexual proposal"; "Look-alike substance—Any substance which by appearance, representation, or manner of distribution would lead a reasonable person to believe that the substance is an illegal drug . . ."; "Disorderly conduct—an act done in an unreasonable manner so as to alarm or disturb others and which provokes a breach of the peace."

Of course, the growing heft of the book speaks only to the failure of officials to really grasp the adolescent and misbehaving imagination, which is both expansive and limitless—it knows no bounds. General commandments such as "Be courteous" and "Dress properly" are both obvious and hopelessly vague; more specific demands—"No running," "No bullying," "No display of gang affiliation" are also vague—thank goodness for that retained "administrative flexibility." As Lao Tzu says in the *Tao Te Ching*, "The more laws you make, the more lawbreakers there will be." But the grownups want to appear serious, and, as is often the case, we don't quite get it: The more crimes you catalog, the more ideas you generate; the more sins you name, the more heave into view.

The little prison administrators expect neither uniform compliance nor automatic submission from every inmate—hence, the elaborate mechanisms for uprooting deviance, for hammering each one into a model prisoner: obedient, compliant, conforming. It begins with the near-universal assumption that schools are in the business of sorting and labeling—winners and losers, smart and stupid, good and bad. Of course, school people are careful not to be so crude—the kinder and gentler employ euphemisms with a medical ring (ADD; BD; TAG) or the sounds of science ("problem with impulse control"). The fog machine is operating at full force, but let just a little air into the room and it comes to this: The good and the smart will walk the runway to the winner's circle, the bad and the stupid will be cast down and out—losers forever. This is a foundational lesson that practically every school teaches to everybody every day.

Another basic lesson is this: School learning is a commodity, traded at the market like boots and hammers. Unlike boots and hammers, whose value is grasped directly and intuitively, the value and use of school learning is elusive and indirect—hence, students are asked to accept its unspecified value on faith. The value of school learning, we're assured, has been calculated precisely by wise and accomplished people, and the masters know better than anyone what's best. "Take this medicine," students are told over and over again, day after tedious day, "it's good for you." Refuse the bitter pill, and go stand in the corner—where all the other losers are assembled. Of course, if you were to point out that lots of dropouts did okay for themselves—Abraham Lincoln and Thomas Jefferson and Ben Franklin for starters; Herman Melville, Mark Twain, Joseph Conrad, and Margaret Mead as well; and John D. Rockefeller

and Andrew Carnegie for good measure—you'd be called an impudent trou-
blemaker, and put in the corner for sure.

§

There have been plenty of attempts in the past to involve students, to create problem-posing curriculum, to support students in thinking and acting.
Herbert Kliebard describes how these efforts have been routinely attacked.[11]
During the Great Depression, progressive educator Harold Rugg[12] wrote
Man and His Changing Society, a well-received history textbook that was real-
istic, faced contradictions, and looked at history through multiple lenses,
including geography, sociology, and economics.

By the 1940s, Rugg's book was attacked by anti-communist list-makers,
Daughters of Colonial Wars, the National Association of Manufacturers,
and the American Legion. They charged that it was anti-American and that
it "tried to give the child an unbiased viewpoint instead of teaching him real
Americanism."

Orlen K. Armstrong, a Hearst newspaper columnist, wrote a long series
attacking Rugg. In one piece entitled "Treason in the Textbooks," Armstrong
concluded that the real purposes of the books were:

1. To present a new interpretation of history in order to "debunk" our heroes
    and cast doubt upon their motives, their patriotism, and their service to
    mankind
2. To cast aspersions on our Constitution and our form of government, and
    shape opinions favorable to replacing them with socialistic control
3. To condemn the American system of private ownership and enterprise,
    and form opinions favorable to collectivism
4. To mold opinions against traditional religious faiths and ideas of morality,
    as being parts of an outgrown system.[13]

When the Soviets launched the Sputnik satellite in 1957, the U.S. military
establishment moved into education in a big way. Admiral Hyman Rickover
went on a speaking tour, attacking the softness of the American curriculum,
arguing for a course of study that would produce the scientists the United
States needed to confront the apparent threat from Soviet science. And the
National Defense Education Act put science curriculum in the hands of the
Pentagon.

In the 1980s and '90s, the right took up the cultural offensive with the Cultural Literacy diatribes by E. D. Hirsch, the unitary elite culture favored by Arthur Schlesinger, and the scolding moral lectures by William Bennett. All of these forces sought to prescribe the class agenda—and they received a sympathetic hearing from most politicians and school superintendents.

The overt or proclaimed curriculum of schools—the disciplines and subjects, the classes and the readings—is only half the matter. The hidden curriculum—all the unstated assumptions, beliefs, and values that prop up the culture and the structure of every school—works its own mighty will. Because it's opaque, unavailable for comment or critique, it is often a more powerful teacher than the official and planned curriculum. Here, for example, is Neil Postman on the essential teachings of the hidden curriculum:

- Passive acceptance is a more desirable response to ideas than active criticism.
- Discovering knowledge is beyond the power of students and is, in any case, none of their business.
- Recall is the highest form of intellectual achievement, and the collection of unrelated "facts" is the goal of education.
- The voice of authority is to be trusted and valued more than independent judgment.
- One's own ideas and those of one's classmates are inconsequential.
- Feelings are irrelevant in education.
- There is always a single, unambiguous Right Answer to a question.
- English is not History and History is not Science and Science is not Art and Art is not Music, and Art and Music are minor subjects and English, History and Science are major subjects, and a subject is something you "take" and, when you have taken it, you have "had" it, and if you have "had" it, you are immune and need not take it again. The Vaccination Theory of Education?[14]

And here, Ivan Illich:

The traditional hidden curriculum of school demands that people of a certain age assemble in groups of about thirty under the authority of a professional teacher for from five hundred to a thousand times a year. It does not matter if the teacher is authoritarian so long as it is the teacher's authority that counts; it does not matter if all meetings occur in the same place so long as they are somehow understood as attendance. The hidden curriculum of school requires—whether by law or by fact—that a citizen accumulate a minimum quantum of school years in order to obtain his civil rights.[15]

. . . The hidden curriculum teaches all children that economically valuable knowledge is the result of professional teaching and that social entitlements depend on the rank achieved in a bureaucratic process. The hidden curriculum transforms the explicit curriculum into a commodity and makes its acquisition the securest form of wealth. . . .

The translation of the need for learning into the demand for schooling and the conversion of the quality of growing up into the price tag of a professional treatment changes the meaning of "knowledge" from a term that designates intimacy, intercourse, and life experience into one that designates professionally packaged products, marketable entitlements, and abstract values. Schools have helped to foster this translation.

The hidden curriculum leads to thinking like this from the vice chancellor at a major university, a respected institution of higher learning: "I have an advanced degree in communications, but that doesn't qualify me to comment on the New York Philharmonic." No? Pity all of us: We must wait passively for some authority to tell us what is right and proper to think who has an advanced degree in . . . what? Appreciation? Composition? Performance? Everything chopped to bits, the cult of the certified expert perched atop a single arid domain.

Another thing that's central to the hidden curriculum is this: Official, certified learning is boring. And school is boring, too, not by accident, but by design. No one really believes anymore that all kids will learn the same things in the same ways at the same time, nor that discrete bits of information poured into the heads of inert youngsters will add up to an education, but the boring system grinds on and on. The big wheel keeps on turning.

Everyone knows that school is boring. We know it, you know it. Because you're reading this page, you likely succeeded in school—and in order to have done so you submitted to a lot of boring stuff. The work was stupid or irrelevant; repetitive or disconnected—not all of it, and not all the time, but let's face it: Much of it, much of the time was boring. It was an endurance test and those who demonstrated that endurance, those whose parents and community taught them how to fake interest while staring at the clock, made it through. And yet you or your family or your community, or all that and more, convinced you that if you put up with all the crap that you couldn't stand, if you went along and played by the rules, there would be a payoff someday, and look, here you are. You submitted, you were bored; you ingested the hidden curriculum, and it's part of you (and us).

Imagine a curriculum project that raised the hidden curriculum, the mechanisms of control, and school boredom as objects of study. We could, as always, begin with questions:

- Is school boring? In what ways? All the time and for each of us the same? What makes it so? Are there alternatives?
- Let's read the Uniform Discipline Code together: Who wrote it? Why? Do other institutions have written codes? What do they say? Are they useful?
- What is the "hidden curriculum?" What unstated assumptions drive the school? Can we state them plainly? Are there any we would change?

§

Zayd Dohrn, a college writing teacher, visited Attica prison in upstate New York several years ago. As he walked into the visitor's entrance, the guards checked his ID and asked him to sign in, first in the log book at the visitor's entrance, then again at the main prison building, and finally at the check-in desk. He walked through a metal detector and had his hand stamped with ultraviolet ink, which was then scanned as he passed through a series of gates on his way to the visiting room, where he finally sat at a small round table under the eyes of a guard on a raised platform and several dozen cameras installed in the ceiling. This is all standard procedure for entering a maximum-security prison, and so none of these requirements should come as a surprise.

Much of this official scrutiny, of course, has become routine in government buildings, in airports, and in malls and offices. What should be, if no longer a surprise, at least a point of curiosity and scrutiny, if not outrage and resistance, is the extent to which schools, in their growing focus on and obsession with surveillance, "tracking," in both senses of the word, "zero tolerance" rules, and "rigorous standards" of both behavior and performance, have come to resemble prisons, and are in fact undermining their putative educational mission. Their deployment of surveillance techniques and their treatment of the bodies and minds under their control can actually destroy the possibility of learning.

Shortly after his prison visit, Dohrn discovered an article innocuously titled "The Art of Safe School Planning: 40 Ways to Manage and Control Student Disruptions," in which Ronald Stephens, the executive director of the National School Safety Center, recommends that schools implement a laundry list of surveillance and disciplinary techniques, ranging from (#1) "Control Campus Access," to (#7) "Establish a state-of-the-art emergency communications center," to (#22) "Remove posters from all windows." Stephens throws in the whole enchilada: "electromagnetic door locking systems," "microdot systems," "surveillance cameras," "detention classrooms . . . for behaviorally disruptive students [equipped with] emergency buzzers or call buttons," as well as "routine locker checks," and "allowing only clear plastic or mesh book bags, or no book bags at all."[16] Stephens represents an ascendant viewpoint on school safety, architecture, and administration: Students in today's schools must be observed, documented, and categorized constantly, their daily lives and activities subjected to prison-like scrutiny and regimentation, all of it, of course, in the name of "safety," "standards," and even, oh my, "the War on Terror."

Dohrn noted that despite the increasing use of disciplinary techniques in schools, the prison analogy breaks down in one significant way: Teachers are not prison guards, and our highest aspiration is not summed up in a single word: *control*. Teachers, then, positioned as both subjects and objects of school surveillance, are uniquely situated to help students develop a critical awareness of, and perhaps even some potential lines of resistance to, the technology of power in today's maximum-security schools. Teachers can take the prison and the analogy as objects of study.

In *Discipline and Punish,* Michel Foucault, the French philosopher and historian, analyzes the measures taken in the 17th century to combat the plague, a new threat that was lethal, invisible, and highly contagious. This was when a new kind of disciplinary power was implemented, an approach that not only isolated a town or village in which an outbreak had occurred, but brought a group of people under intense scrutiny and segmentation, confining residents to their homes, placing sentinels at the corners of streets and intersections, and requiring regular review and registration of the position, condition, and identity of each individual under quarantine. To Foucault, the plague and the model of the quarantine led to the discovery of a new type or "technology of power" that he called "discipline."

For Foucault, a "mechanism of discipline"[17] can be thought of as any "enclosed, segmented space, observed at every point, in which the individuals are inserted in a fixed place, in which the slightest movements are supervised, in which all events are recorded, in which uninterrupted links exist between the center and periphery."[18] The "architectural figure" of this disciplinary power is Jeremy Bentham's "Panopticon," a model prison built upon a simple concept with echoing and accelerating implications: a tower surrounded by a ring of cells. A guard stands in the central tower; he can observe each of the prisoners, but they can neither see him nor one another; prisoners never know when or how they are being observed, but recognize at all times their own visibility and vulnerability: "Hence the major effect of the Panopticon: to induce in the inmate a state of conscious and permanent visibility that assures the automatic functioning of power."[19]

The Panopticon has become a basic model or technology of power in our society. What Foucault calls "The swarming of disciplinary mechanisms" ensures that disciplinary powers "have a certain tendency to become de-institutionalized, to emerge from the closed fortresses in which they once functioned and to circulate in a 'free' state."[20] In other words, what begins as an effort to regulate and control certain marginal or dangerous segments of the population—victims of the plague, prisoners, the insane—becomes a technology used to normalize the population as a whole, adopted by all institutions with any interest whatsoever in control. "Is it surprising," asks Foucault rhetorically, "that prisons resemble factories, schools, barracks, hospitals, which all resemble prisons?"[21]

Efforts to implement surveillance techniques and disciplinary power in schools have been going on for years, of course, but the process was dramatically accelerated in this country by two events: first, the shootings at Columbine High School in 1999, which provoked widespread worry over a supposed trend of school violence, and second, the attacks of 9/11, which sparked a similar nationwide panic over "terrorism" and a drive, not just in schools but in every facet of American life, toward "security" of the homeland, the school, the workplace, the neighborhood, and everything else. Foucault's emphasis on the origins of discipline during the plague is instructive here, as school violence, not to mention terrorism, is often figured as a metaphorical plague, something "contagious," "invisible," and "lethal." Foucault reminds us that "Behind the disciplinary mechanism can be read the haunting memory of 'contagions', of the plague . . . of people who appear and disappear, live and die in disorder."[22]

In response to the widely publicized shootings at Columbine, and in the grip of a national paranoia about terrorism, schools across the country have adopted new policies and technologies to make them "safe," or perhaps simply to give the illusion of safety, the comfort of feeling safer, and this despite the fact that school violence has actually been trending downward over the past decade, with junior high school and high school crime rates, including the rates of serious violent crimes, declining between 1992 and 2008. Despite this decline, the use of surveillance technologies and other disciplinary techniques has increased, including a jump in the number of schools using surveillance cameras from 39 to 48% in the 2-year period following 9/11. Schools are sinking more and more of their money into "security" while cutting budgets, dramatically narrowing the curriculum, eliminating programs in sports, music, the arts, and more. Interestingly, although data and proof are demanded whenever a curricular innovation is proposed, there is no such requirement when the question is security. So let's ask: What's the evidence that the security systems being imported and stuffed into schools makes them safer? What besides hardware makes us safe?

School architecture has increasingly been renovated or redesigned with an emphasis on surveillance. Mark Lam, managing partner of a large school facility design firm, suggests that "surveillance can be incorporated in two ways—actual and perceived. Crime is reduced as surveillance (or the perception) is increased. . . . [School facilities] should provide views for maximum surveillance from as few control points as possible." Lam suggests that schools "avoid circular or zigzag-shaped hallways" and "remove restroom doors . . . to reduce horseplay and vandalism." Some schools have taken the Panopticon model to its logical extreme, designing buildings so that one person, presumably the school principal, can stand in his or her office and have an unobstructed view of the entire facility. The message: I can see you.

Of course, new technologies allow the architectural model of the Panopticon to be extended much further, almost indefinitely—the venetian blinds that Bentham imagined in the central tower of his Panopticon to hide the guard from the prisoners in the outside ring have been replaced by the ubiquitous black globes covering security cameras that can be wired into local police stations, projecting the unobstructed gaze of state power directly into the school hallways. Some schools have created more Orwellian projects, including pilot programs in Radio Frequency Identification (RFID) programs, which put electronic tags on student IDs in order to trace their movements on a central computerized map. Other schools use GPS technology to shadow bus fleets, metal detectors and bomb-sniffing dogs at entryways, and fingerprint readers and biometric hand scans to track attendance and library withdrawals.

In such an environment, teachers can easily and routinely become instruments of disciplinary surveillance, tracking students, labeling, observing, categorizing, and disciplining them. We do it—policing student work for signs of potential violence, extracting feelings and motives from creative expressions and comparing these motives against a battery of normalized prescriptions in our heads—and we read or hear stories of the more extreme examples: teachers who report students to the police or even the Secret Service for perceived violent threats gleaned from school journals or homework assignments.

On the other hand, we are often ourselves the objects of disciplinary surveillance: the cameras, background checks, urine tests, and "professional evaluation" systems that categorize, fix, and supervise us in our everyday activities. And the moment our roles are switched, we teachers begin to model the typical resistance behavior of a recalcitrant high school student—slouching and doing other work during staff meetings, making off-color jokes about authority figures, resisting surveillance and feedback. There are also the disciplinary procedures of standardized curricula and "No Child Left Behind"; we are subject to random checks by education officials who can show up in our classrooms at any time and physically check students' workbooks to make sure we've reached the required page for a specified date. Such surveillance constitutes an example of the way in which disciplinary power draws teachers as well as students into its field, and also the way that surveillance intervenes in the teacher-student relationship, and in the pedagogical process itself.

An article by Henry Fountain in the *New York Times* entitled "The Camera Never Blinks, but It Multiplies" is accompanied by a creepy lineup of photos of surveillance cameras and the street scenes they're recording. "It's spring," Fountain begins, practically chirping, "and a new crop of police surveillance cameras is sprouting in cities big and small. New York is installing 500 on street corners; Chicago is upgrading several thousand; and even the city of Dillingham, Alaska, has 80—one for every 30 residents."[23] The ones in Chicago can be seen high up on the telephone polls patrolling the territory of the poor, their bright blue lights—a nod to the ACLU—blinking wildly 24/7.

Fountain carefully points out the many modern accoutrements: "These newer cameras can pan, tilt and zoom, and are networked through the Internet, so video images can be viewed and stored centrally." Paid for, of course, with "homeland security" funds. But there is a downside: "It is impossible for a police department to continuously monitor 2,000, 500 or even, in the case of Dillingham, 80 cameras. So other than producing mountains of visual data—and raising the inevitable questions of privacy—how useful are they?" Of course, law enforcement argues that "just putting up a camera in plain sight can deter crime." Law enforcement officials imagine "a future in which software will analyze video for possible signs of terrorist activity, like someone placing a suitcase in front of a building."[24]

This brave new world of visibility and vulnerability provoked Zayd Dohrn to give an assignment to his writing students that was designed to make Panopticism itself a focus of study, a problem to be investigated. He asked his students, after reading a bit from Foucault, to photograph, and then to write about, mechanisms of discipline that they can see or uncover in their own daily lives. Students chose to photograph disciplinary institutions ranging from police stations to hospitals, from schools to grocery stores, airports and buses, and in one case, the student's own family. They also took pictures of their cellphones, computers, credit cards, lunchroom passes, and IDs.

The assignment, predictably, caused a certain amount of institutional friction. Banks, airports, and shopping malls take offense at someone photographing the security cameras, two-way mirrors, guards, and records that enable their hyper-surveillance. It is one of the great ironies of our society that observing and documenting the very apparatus that constantly observes and documents us is unacceptable and sometimes illegal. Two students were taken into the basement security room at a local shopping mall and interrogated by the store managers about why they were photographing the store's cameras. They explained that it was a homework assignment, and pointed out that the security cameras, after all, were photographing *them* without *their* permission. The manager responded that photographing the security cameras was threatening and potentially dangerous. "There are terrorists around," he told them. "We're watching so that we can protect you. You simply can't watch us watching you." A perfect Foucaultian moment.

The point, of course, is not to get students into trouble, and this assignment was meant simply as one attempt to start a conversation. But posing disciplinary power and surveillance as a problem in the classroom and a question to be interrogated can be productive for teachers as well as students—it allows for active critical engagement with the world, including the mechanisms of control that are all around us. "You simply can't watch us watching you"—this is all the provocation we need for active interrogation and engaged curriculum.

The prisoner in Foucault's Panopticon is always "the object of information, never the subject of communication."[25] It is our job as teachers to challenge that: Our students must become the subjects of communication, actors in their own dramas and writers of their own scripts, even as we ourselves resist being transformed into objects by the mechanisms of surveillance that so profoundly define the modern educational institution.

In schools shot through with mechanisms of disciplinary surveillance, the technology of power might itself constitute some part of the humanizing curriculum. Students can think critically about disciplinary power, about how they are being watched, by whom, and for what purpose. They can question, and they can act. By questioning and acting ourselves, we can show them how it's done.

§

Paulo Freire argues that

> Education as the practice of freedom—as opposed to education as the practice of domination—denies that man is abstract, isolated, independent, and unattached to the world; it also denies that the world exists as a reality apart from people. Authentic reflection considers neither abstract man nor the world without people, but people in their relations with the world.[26]

As teachers, we can work to find ways to engage students with their own situations; we can pose problems that might allow them to consider their vivid and essential places in the world. In that way, in this corner of this school or classroom, in this unique place—in this open space we are constructing together—people will begin to experience themselves as powerful authors of their own narratives, luminous actors in their own dramas, the essential creators of their own lives. They will find ways to articulate their own desires and demands and questions. In this space everyone will live *in search of* rather than *in accordance with* or *in accommodation to.*

This is teaching designed to develop free minds in free people. This, too, is teaching the taboo.

TWO.

Make Conflict Visible: The Darkness in Our Own Hearts

> They were conquerors, and for that you want only brute force—nothing to boast of, when you have it, since your strength is just an accident arising from the weakness of others. They grabbed what they could get for the sake of what was to be got. It was just robbery with violence, aggravated murder on a great scale, and men going at it blind—as is very proper for those who tackle a darkness. The conquest of the earth, which mostly means the taking it away from those who have a different complexion or slightly flatter noses than ourselves, is not a pretty thing when you look into it too much. What redeems it is the idea only. An idea at the back of it; not a sentimental pretence but an idea; and an unselfish belief in the idea—something you can set up, and bow down before, and offer a sacrifice to.
>
> —Joseph Conrad, *Heart of Darkness*[27]

Joseph Conrad's *Heart of Darkness* begins with a group of Englishmen sitting on a boat on the Thames River in London. In one class, at one school, during one semester some years ago, the events in this chapter happened. Let this be an invitation to your own voyage. As the class read the first lines, "The Nellie, a cruising yawl, swung to her anchor without a flutter of the sails, and was at rest," a few students laughed with recognition—not because cruising yawls or sails were part of their world, but because Nelly was one of the reigning rap artists of the day. Clearly, Conrad had not named the boat in honor of the rap star, but that's how everyone reads, making sense and making links, and here the students were making their own meaning, their own connections to their special contemporary spaces. Someone called out, "Make sure you ask the name of the boat on the quiz," and everyone laughed again, as if we would be reading toward a *Jeopardy*-type conclusion. We would be venturing into something much deeper and darker than quizzes, but the students couldn't know that now—pits and caves, lion's dens, and more lurked just over the horizon.

Maxine Greene says that life has to be more than one damn thing after another, and yet the idea that teaching English is just one damn book after another has a powerful grip on our collective thinking. "Here's the curriculum for freshman English," the department chair declares at a staff meeting as he hands out a short list of appropriate books, copies of which are to be found in the book room, and everyone dutifully looks it over. A list of books: one damn thing after another.

All higher aspirations feel suddenly lofty and romantic, and yet we all know that what goes on in class is often quite different from what is expected or planned—class is always part blood sport, part group therapy, part political debate, part jaw-dropping awe, and part regret. The regrets are always there, for the conversations are forever unfinished, the depths unplumbed, the echoes of the many things that didn't happen resounding.

Although the list of books may be an odd way to regard curriculum, it's not completely worthless. The revolutionary artist-author Junot Diaz describes the challenge and possibilities of books as a matter of embarking on a path of discovery, a journey that values questions, as opposed to the path of punishment in which someone pounces every time a student fails to offer up the desired answers. Diaz argues that in a world organized around competition, the act of reading is revolutionary—it creates compassion, it demands that we look at the world from the point of view of another. Moreover, reading creates human beings as it undermines the narcissistic myth that we are entirely awesome, that we always win, that we deserve all the stuff we have. It lets us recognize that we are vulnerable, flawed, contradictory, and petty. But, in addition to making us face that, it reminds us that we are beautiful, worthy of love, and extraordinarily important.

Dr. Seuss says, "Oh, the places you'll go, the wonders you'll see," and sometimes digging to the back of the book storage room yields long-retired texts. That happened with *Heart of Darkness*—a few dusty class sets in faded red covers, hidden and uncovered, just on an instinct that maybe the old imperialist could light the kids up.

Of course, there are all kinds of problems with a text like Conrad's, not the least of which is the fact that it is the classic and much-maligned Dead

White Man writing about the Continent at the height of the "scramble for Africa" at the end of the 19th century. But the book was on the approved list, and it was a chance to go beyond the perennial *Things Fall Apart* by Chinua Achebe, which is the only African literature most American high school kids will ever see. We would read Conrad and then African authors, from Lumumba and Tati-Loutard to Achebe's critique of *Heart of Darkness*.

Right away, Conrad draws a startling analogy. The narrator, Marlowe, describes how the Roman invaders must have been frightened, terrified of the "natives" 2 millennia ago when they encountered the tribes of Anglos and Saxons along the Thames River right there in what would become Great Britain:

> I was thinking of very old times, when the Romans first came here, nineteen hundred years ago—the other day. . . . darkness was here yesterday. Imagine the feelings of a commander of a fine—what d'ye call 'em?—trireme in the Mediterranean, ordered suddenly to the north; run overland across the Gauls in a hurry; put in charge of one of these craft the legionaries—a wonderful lot of handy men they must have been, too—used to build, apparently by the hundred, in a month or two, if we may believe what we read. Imagine him here—the very end of the world, a sea the colour of lead, a sky the colour of smoke, a kind of ship about as rigid as a concertina—and going up this river with stores, or orders, or what you like. Sandbanks, marshes, forests, savages— precious little to eat fit for a civilized man, nothing but Thames water to drink. No Falernian wine here, no going ashore. Here and there a military camp lost in a wilderness, like a needle in a bundle of hay—cold, fog, tempests, disease, exile, and death—death skulking in the air, in the water, in the bush. They must have been dying like flies here. Oh, yes—he did it. Did it very well, too, no doubt, and without thinking much about it either, except afterwards to brag of what he had gone through in his time, perhaps. They were men enough to face the darkness. And perhaps he was cheered by keeping his eye on a chance of promotion to the fleet at Ravenna by and by, if he had good friends in Rome and survived the awful climate. Or think of a decent young citizen in a toga—perhaps too much dice, you know—coming out here in the train of some prefect, or tax-gatherer, or trader even, to mend his fortunes. Land in a swamp, march through the woods, and in some inland post feel the savagery, the utter savagery, had closed round him—all that mysterious life of the wilderness that stirs in the forest, in the jungles, in the hearts of wild men. There's no initiation either into such mysteries. He has to live in the midst of the incomprehensible, which is also detestable. And it has a fascination, too, that goes to work upon him. The fascination of the abomination—you know, imagine the growing regrets, the longing to escape, the powerless disgust, the surrender, the hate.

Marlowe pauses and describes the logic of imperial conquest: "They grabbed what they could get for the sake of what was to be got. It was just robbery with violence, aggravated murder on a great scale, and men going at it blind. . . ."

What the hell is Conrad saying? Imagine the critique here, for he is about to tell us about the Belgian project of imperialist extraction from the Congo. And he starts with a comparison to how it must have been for Roman imperialists to try to control the island of England. What an indictment! The indigenous people were to be scorned and killed, their culture considered the ultimate darkness and evil, their resources there for the taking, for "It was just robbery with violence, aggravated murder on a great scale, and men going at it blind." And the language: This is a language of domination, the binary between those in imperial control and those who are defined as alien others, dangerous outsiders. Today, we see this language in the everyday expressions of the master discourse: savage, predatory, vicious. People who do not conform to our kind of political formations are in tribes (whether it is Afghanistan or an echo of Native Americans); pharmacy conglomerates are corporations, medical marijuana collectives are "cartels." The list of banned types goes on and on and on: warlords, kingpins, insurgents, gangs, rebels.

This is a precise and crystal-clear description of the depredations of imperialism. And then the insight that perhaps this Roman captain had come to the colony to mend his fortune after having lost it at gambling—the colony, then as now, as the site an adventurer must brave to recoup his treasury, whether investing in African diamond mines or buying Section Eight housing in Harlem. Connections, connections . . .

Certainly, the trope of savagery and the need to tame or suppress the savage is central to the project of schooling itself. James Isdell, Protector of Aborigines in Western Australia in the first decade of the 20th century, commenting on the forcible removal of native children to boarding schools, noted that he wouldn't hesitate for a moment, for this was a humane project to rid them of their savagery, and that no matter how intense the momentary grief of their mothers, "They soon forget their offspring." After all, they are not human in the same sense that we are.

The famous Carlisle Indian School in Pennsylvania reveals this drive most cruelly in the testimony of its founder, Colonel Richard Pratt, before Congress:

> A great general has said that the only good Indian is a dead one, and that high sanction of this destruction has been an enormous factor in promoting Indian

massacres. In a sense, I agree with the sentiment, but only in this: that all the Indian there is in the race should be dead. Kill the Indian in him, save the man.[28]

Pratt played a similar role to that of reformers such as General Samuel Armstrong, who founded Hampton Institute in 1868 for the uplifting (and civilizing) of Black workers in Virginia. A few years after Hampton opened, Pratt wrote,

> This is no easy machine to run wisely, rightly. The darkies are so full of human nature and have to be most carefully watched over. They are apt to be possessed with strange notions. To simply control them is one thing, but to educate, to draw them out, to develop the germ of good possibilities into firm fruition, requires the utmost care.[29]

So, on one day, in one classroom, begins a political reading of *Heart of Darkness*, a story that describes in unsparing detail the horrors of the imperialist project. As Marlowe's little ship first approaches the coast of Africa, it passes a French warship that is standing off shore, simply lobbing cannon shells into the jungle. Making war on nature—an affecting, surreal image. Of course, the scary jungle, the alien neighborhood or the dangerous river, the forbidding plants and animals, represent the fear of nature, and the notion in the European mind that the African *is* nature, the unrepressed *id.* The failure of Europe to complete the colonization of Africa for 200 years is explained by this myth of the dangerous jungle. Here is the stance of Europe toward Africa: worthy of bombing and killing, of extraction and exploitation, and nothing more.

The students read a chapter from Kirkpatrick Sale's *The Conquest of Paradise*[30] in which he describes the fear of nature that is central to Western culture, from the Bible on. He analyzes the attitude of Europeans to the peoples and ecology of America when they arrived. But the same analysis explains much of the Africa project on the European agenda.

They begin to argue about whether or not Conrad, this White guy, could do a decent job of explaining Africa and the European penetration. The answer was not so easy. Clearly, he failed to capture, he could not understand, the inside of African cultures. Yet Conrad certainly had experience with imperialism, with the mechanics, the politics, and the psychology of colonial expansion.

As they read on, it's clear that Conrad's initial indictment of empire's organized theft only deepens. Indeed, Marlowe must discover that everything he feared and loathed about Africa was deep inside the Europeans themselves. The heart of darkness, the horror, is *us*. There is no more thorough or powerful indictment of imperialism written by a European in fiction than *Heart of Darkness.*

The class begins to read historians and political analysts from the period. How have they described the colonial venture into Africa, the workings of imperialism? In short, they did a horrible job. These accounts, even by liberals who found fault with the project, were flat, uninformed, and inevitably self-satisfied about the advanced status of Western culture. Only the artist, the one who looks deeply, stands up through time. Conrad unmasks a phenomenon—from fear of nature to sexual repression to vile and rampaging White supremacy—that is perhaps more complex and profound than he himself could fully grasp as he was writing it. That's the power of deep art: It can capture complex reality in a way that will surely resonate and be read differently in different times.

In a sense, the text is like a new dance step. The dance itself is interesting, but of course, it only exists when we dance it. And each generation does the dance differently. This class is a group of new readers—urban students, a diverse mix of races and classes. For some, this is the first novel they had read seriously, read and considered with a group of their peers. As when you learn to dance, you get out there at first tentatively. You dance it a little bit; then you feel more comfortable, you inhabit the dance, you bring your own interpretation. You're not making up the novel by bringing your own reading to it, but you grapple with it as well as you can with the tools and consciousness you have. You are the one the author gave clues to for a field of interpretation. Everything we saw in Conrad was surely there—just as some moves on the dance floor are ridiculous, some are clearly interpretations of the dance—but perhaps it waited for this class to dust the books off from the bookroom for this reading to come to light.

This particular group of students is bringing a particular modern reading to the book. That much is inevitable. Every person and each generation reads it differently. Harold Bloom says that Shakespeare's power is that he reads us as we read him. Or, as Coleridge said, we are inscribing the text along with Shakespeare as we read it. This is not simply a matter of bringing our prejudices and narrowness to the reading. It is the text existing in the context of our society and particularly in the context of this classroom, a group of 11th graders, half of them African American, in an urban school, in the months after the 9/11 attacks.

It is interesting to see the margin writing that students had done the last time the book was read, 25 or 30 years before. Nothing is there about political analysis. There are notes like "symbol for death" next to the account of the old woman knitting in the shipping office; "fear, death" next to image of darkness; "foreshadowing" next to a description of the outfitting of the ship for the trip to the African coast. Whoever taught the book before led students through it with apparently slight reference to African people, to colonialism, to the political violence at the core of the text. Every teacher's experience, of course, colors the reading—the eye of the war resister versus the daughter of the 1950s who'd imbibed New Criticism—and so does every student's. These were kids of color in a globalizing world, and they tore into the political core, fought to find the African point of view.

This, of course, was to be a disappointment. Conrad knew little about the Africans, like all Europeans of the time. And the narrow, stereotypic, racist depictions of Africans as they are glimpsed during the voyage and encountered at the end are characterizations from the mouth of Marlow, the boat captain, the narrator. All Conrad is telling us is that, indeed, White people think like this, White people talk like this. It's the same strategy Mark Twain employs in his meditation on race in America, *Huckleberry Finn.* He puts the racist words in the mouth of the narrator, Huck. But Huck is ultimately disillusioned and disgusted with White "civilization."

Many parents are outraged by Huck Finn, and Chinua Achebe denounces *Heart of Darkness*—they want Black characters more three-dimensional and White people perhaps a bit more humane, more decent, more, well, anti-racist. The bad news that Twain and Conrad bring is that this is what White people are really like. By being such unvarnished truth-tellers, they get everyone upset. But in the case of these two authors at least, they do it as part of a project to expose and denounce the problem, the genocidal sickness that constitutes respectable White culture. They each use this doubling, the voice of a narrator steeped in racism, to expose racism.

The truly subversive thing about Huck Finn, the returning image that would have Huck thumbing his nose at the current education authorities and cultural powers, is his rejection of White civilization. Indeed, Huck tries, he tries valiantly, to enter White society and be a racist like everyone else. But, by being drawn into Jim's escape along with his own, he just can't make it as a White boy. Indeed, every time he tries to be with White people, on the plantations or the villages along the river, he finds them hellish and insanely violent. He has to go against his god, his family, and the state to declare that he'd finally decided to do the right thing even if it meant going to hell.

Toni Morrison[31] takes Twain to the ultimate implications of his brutal representation of White consciousness. She deals not just with the center of *Huckleberry Finn*, the humanizing story of Huck's journey from brutal white civilization to his rebellion in solidarity with Jim. She examines the puzzling ending, in which Jim is freed but Tom and Huck continue to toy with him and even torment him. She emphasizes that White people are revealed to define their freedom, their sense of possibility, in relation to Black enslavement and oppression. She describes this reality stunningly as the "parasitical nature of white freedom."[32] Can we teach that? Can we really face that through literature? Certainly, to try to cover up the horrifying truths with platitudes about children's adventures, about "how they spoke back then," would be a literary crime not worthy of honest classrooms.

Huck Finn is all about truth and lies, deceptions and propaganda. Twain is building a case against the silent assertion (i.e., the hegemonic consciousness of the time) that slavery is normal. What a powerful journey to take with students—if we face it honestly and together. We live in a society that tries to hide things from young people and that lives by "silent assertions" of the way things are. Helping students develop critical literacy in order to empower them to get around the hidden is about what David Bradley calls *decoding signifiers*.

We could choose to read European and American novels— novels which never use the N-word, which seemingly have no relationship to race, like Jane Austen or Henry James. But Toni Morrison and Edward Said have both shown that in these novels, too, the subtext, the context, the elephant in the room, is the colonial foundations of the edifice of the societies in which White people live. Perhaps we would be less offended initially to read the tales of White gentry in Austen or White society parties in James. The books are simply about other things than colonialism. But in reality, they are never completely or innocently about "other things." The conquest of Africa, the wealth built on slave labor, the continuing tribute from the colonies—these are realties that suffuse Western life and literature.

Conrad and Twain rub our faces in it. Twain pisses the reader off; James doesn't. Which is truer? Really, we could start from any text, classic or modern, part of the new or old canon. If we can get deeply enough into it, if we can make meaning of it, if we encounter something new and bring something old, we will be both subversive and reverent. We will be changed by it.

And a high school class can go deeper, go further. We read the powerful and insightful works of African authors, not only Achebe, Amos Tutuola, and Ngugi Wa Thiong'o, but revolutionaries and theoreticians such as Franz

Fanon and Amilcar Cabral. And from there we go on to other continents, other communities.

The struggle for a voice, the struggle to assert one's very being, suffuses literary texts from the beginning. Shakespeare poses as the quintessential European, fascinated and intrigued by the "others" who are enslaved in Africa and encountered in the Americas. He creates Caliban in *The Tempest* as the embodiment of the slave-indigenous person, a semi-monster. But Caliban is also a great rebel, one who fights back, even as he is obtaining an education from the Europeans (who imagine that the indigenous language is not a language at all—a familiar trope). Caliban spits at Prospero, "You taught me language, and my profit on't is, I know how to curse. The red plague rid you for learning me your language." Prospero gladly tortures and torments Caliban, his slave, whose name is a rearrangement of cannibal, but he explains to his daughter that we Europeans need him, we are dependent on him really, to provide our riches: "We cannot miss him: he does make our fire, fetch in our wood, and serves in offices that profit us."

Nearly 400 years later, Cuban intellectual Roberto Retamar embraces Caliban as the indigenous identity, the dreaded "other" in European eyes.[33] He exposes this tendency in Western culture to demand the civilizing of the "savages" through education and repression. Retamar draws a line from Caliban to the independistas to José Martí to Gabriel Garcia Marquez and away from Latin American writers such as José Sarmiento, the Argentine author who was madly in love with European culture and envious of the North Americans for their extermination of the Indian population.

Indeed, in his play *A Tempest,* Aimé Cesaire, the great founder of Negritude studies, updates *The Tempest* and posits Caliban as a hero and rebel—a Black Power advocate and a genius exposing the idiotic domination fantasies of the Europeans.[34]

Today, subaltern artists are gaining a voice from the margins even as they break down border fences—mixing, collaging, reappropriating, and repurposing the global voices of their world. Junot Diaz slides easily between science fiction, nerd English, Dominican slang, Spanglish, and Western classics. Enrique Chagoya mixes ancient codex paintings depicting the Spanish conquistadors in Mexico with indigenous art and modern comic art. Massive struggles are always reflected in the arts. Those of us in the schools cannot simply share stultified and sanitized texts in the name of objectivity. The arts are one arena of social struggle for our students, and we are lucky to be able to wade into it with them.

Too often, we fail to teach Garcia Marquez, Cesaire, or Diaz. Standard high school fare is William Golding's *Lord of the Flies,* that cautionary tale of the group of British boys stranded on a Pacific island. In an engaging and imaginative story, we find that the boys—absent the civilizing presence of their British parents and teachers—revert to an imagined prehistoric savagery. They create a warrior class, paint their faces, do wild dances to invoke the spirit of the hunt, and then start killing one another. What's wrong with this picture? Students are drawn to wonder about human nature and they often concur that such nature is generally violent and competitive. They can't easily imagine that the violence and competitiveness they see around them is the creation of the current class system, one that we project on other eras and peoples.

Worse yet, the warning is that if we are not careful, we might become like *them*, the dreaded tribal people, the violent, the face-painted, the, well, non-White. Many people did, of course, have ritual dances and many hunted game. But they did not slaughter their fellow villagers with industrial efficiency. That accomplishment awaited the development of civilization. In general, societies with hunting and gathering in the center have been peaceful or, at most, engaged in ritual conflict with minimal killing. The essentially racist core of Golding's novel is the reinforcement of the Western fantasy of its own superiority, of the danger and terror of the savage "other."

This does not mean we should not teach *Lord of the Flies*. Indeed, it is a great jumping-off point for some of the biggest thinking a 9th grader might encounter concerning civilization, human nature, and fundamental values. But we would do well to teach it alongside Kenzaburo Oe's brilliant *Nip the Buds/Shoot the Kids*, the inside/out *Lord of the Flies*. Oe imagines a group of tough kids billeted in the countryside in Japan during World War II, abandoned and left to die. Here, the kids build a community of mutual recognition and support based on a common humanity in sharp contrast to the behavior of the adults who are busy making war on the world and even dropping nuclear bombs on their fellow beings.

The suppression of the savages (in the world and in ourselves) theme runs through Western literature and throughout the education project. Chicago Afrocentric educator Carol Lee unearths the thinking of early psychologists who helped construct school curriculum, such as Stanley Hall, who wrote:

> Among the tribes of Dahomey, . . . and in the Fan, Felup Wolop, Kru, and other strips . . . sometimes resort to cannibalism, use anagglutinative speech, believe profoundly in witchcraft, are lazy, improvident, imitative, fitful, passionate, affectionate, faithful, are devoted to music and rhythm and have always practiced slavery among themselves. . . . polygamy is universal, fecundity is high, and morality great. Strong sex instincts are necessary to preserve the

race. As soon as the child can go it alone, it begins to shift for itself. Stealing is universal and is a game and falsehoods are clever accomplishments. . . . Our slaves came from the long narrow belt, not many miles from the sea. . . . It is surprising to see how few of his aboriginal traits the Negro has lost, although many of them are modified.[35]

We need not police the bookshelves to weed out the offensive texts. Powerful teaching is not so much finding the perfect text—engaging, relevant, inoffensive—for our students. Rather, it is making the entire universe relevant to students as they come to understand that they can read the world and make and remake reality that makes sense to them.

In the end, the Africa unit stretched out for several months. The class created book groups and reported to one another what they learned. At first, the readings were planned to extend throughout Africa, but in the end, they focused on the Congo, where so much that is tragic and hopeful about Africa can be found. The students followed Marlowe's trip up the Congo River with book groups in which five different groups read different authors on the Congo. Here, they gained a broad experience with the Congo in literature through exploring historical studies (Adam Hochschild's *King Leopold's Ghost*), novels (V. S. Naipaul's *A Bend in the River* and Barbara Kingsolver's *Poisonwood Bible*), travel memoirs (Redmond O'Hanlon's *No Mercy: A Journey to the Heart of the Congo*), and criticism (Sven Lindqvist's *Exterminate All the Brutes*). In addition, the whole class read pieces from former president Patrice Lumumba (killed by the CIA and Belgian intelligence), poetry (e.g., Vachel Lindsay's colonialist "Congo" and the works of Tchicaya U Tam'si, Jean-Baptiste Tati-Loutard, and Emmanuel Dongala), and current news and analysis concerning the overthrow of Mobutu and the civil war. Lindqvist's work was particularly striking, as he took off from the attitudes exposed by Conrad, the European notion of nonhuman beasts that must be exterminated. Students kept asking why, and every bit of evidence intensified that propulsive question. What dispositions of mind allowed for the widespread practice and general acceptance of genocide as a colonial commonplace? Why did it work? Why the popularity of eugenics, the "science of race," with its hierarchy of superior and inferior races? Why and how did Conrad develop some sense of a shared and common humanity in the midst of an orgy of self-adulation in the project of conquest and murder? They linked U.S. attempts to wipe out Native Americans as well as Germany's genocide of the Herero people of southwest Africa during Hitler's childhood to the Holocaust as the practice of colonialism brought home to the metropole. And they kept pushing: Why?

Film worked, too, including a 1994 version of *Heart of Darkness,* Raoul Peck's *Lumumba,* and a modern *Heart of Darkness* tale, *Congo,* based on the novel by Michael Crichton. And students watched *Apocalypse Now,* Coppola's attempt to apply the Conrad formula of failed imperial venture to the story of Vietnam.

There was no neat conclusion for this class, and indeed, there could not have been one. Literature, like life, is bottomless; literature, like education, is a site of struggle, both in the writing and in the reading of it. It's a place where we work out the meaning of democracy and construct who we are and who we might yet become, both differently and together. Teachers are not simply decoders, the ones who unlock the secret by revealing the true meaning to the students through teaching concepts such as the "symbol for death" and "foreshadowing." Teaching the taboo consists of making meaning through the encounter of the lives and the values of each of us—teachers and students alike.

§

In protest against the crusty male literary authorities of her day, Virginia Woolf declared: "Literature is no one's private ground; literature is common ground; let us trespass freely and fearlessly and find our own way for ourselves." When teaching is at its best, we seize the texts and seize the time—we change it, and at the same time it changes us.

THREE.

Into the Woods

If you are troubled by the cruelty and violence and lovelessness you
see around you . . . if you've seen people around you pushed around or
crushed . . . if you feel a huge gap between what you're told is going
on and what you actually see and feel on your nerves—then this is the
material of your art, there's no escaping it. The question then is, how do
you make enduring beauty and form out of such materials? And that will
be the question of a lifetime.

—Adrienne Rich, interview

At the sound of the bell, 16-year-old Maya Minter gathered her books
together hastily and headed for the door. It was the first day of class for a
new semester.

"What's the rush?" asked Ms. Gloamen, fifth-period math teacher, peer-
ing over her half-glasses, amused.

"I'm on my way to Avi's World," Maya said, her open, animated face
glowing. "And I don't want to be late."

Ms. Gloamen rolled her eyes and gave a barely perceptible shake of
her head. "Ahhh . . ." she drew out a low audible sigh, the bemused smile
deepening slightly. "Ahhh . . . Avi's World, of course. All roads eventually
lead to Avi's World."

Avi's World is short-hand for a popular elective called "Experiments in
Reading, Literature and the World," the creation of Avi Lessing, an English
teacher with the scooped-out, retro-punk look of a taller, younger, and decidedly Jewish Elvis Costello. The kids all call him Mr. Lessing to his face, but
the class has been Avi's World almost from the start, and over time that title—

always preceded with a sigh of wildly divergent resonances and meanings—has morphed into a metaphorical handle for a whole range of approaches, activities, and states of mind. Ahhh . . . Avi's World.

Avi left the University of Colorado without much of a plan, drifted job to job—waiting tables, of course; working for a friend in retail—and found himself at a multinational in Prague. "I saw *Say Anything*," he says, "and a line delivered by John Cusack summed up my state of mind perfectly." Avi quotes from memory: "I don't want to sell anything that's bought or processed; I don't want to buy anything that's processed or sold; I don't want to process anything that's sold or bought." And then the punchline: "I just want to hang out with your daughter."

Avi returned home hoping to find a way to live his life without buying, selling, or processing. He wanted to hang out with somebody's daughter. Like many others, he backed into teaching.

Avi's classroom is Avi's World—a jumble of books and struggling plants, a collection of carpet fragments and worn-out arm chairs pushed together into the aspiration of a circle. The overhead lights are usually off, the room illuminated by candles and old table lamps as well as the natural light from outdoors.

The work in Avi's World always involves reading an article or book; writing a story or essay; documenting, editing, rethinking, and reconnecting. There's time for discussion, of course, and also meditation, massage, stretching, yoga, and more. At the center of the whole five-ring circus—the generator and point of departure for everything else that happens—is the act of storytelling. As often prompted, provoked, or planned as it is spontaneous and surprising, someone takes center stage each day to read or speak a piece. These occasions become the raw material for vision and revision, for research and writing, for drama and poetry and song.

"All I want to do," Avi says—presumably besides hanging out with somebody's daughter—"is to teach a really good kindergarten class with 18-year-olds." He wants them to know one another's names as a start and then to know something about how the other person feels and experiences life. "Storytelling and listening allows them to see themselves and others beyond categories and cliques, way beyond labels of any kind." Seeing one's own complex and layered motives and meanings, Avi believes, might open kids to seeing others as multidimensional as well, trembling and struggling and real as dirt. Theater is his key: "People need theater," he says. "The drama of our own lives needs to be seen, and the drama of the lives of others needs to be felt." The gangster has not just a heart but a mind; the nerd has a wild imagination and feels both pain and desire.

"Imaginative literature is wonderful, of course," Avi says. "And novels and poetry can take us into all kinds of important places. But for me teaching reading and writing is ultimately unsatisfying if the kids aren't motivated, and they're not motivated as long as we abstract everything, theorize it to death, and keep busy pushing the real stuff of life–all the themes of literature after all–out of our classrooms."

Avi draws a big circle in his notebook. "Look," he says, the pen stabbing the page. "This," he draws a little pie wedge from center to circumference, "is everything we know." He labels it "K." "And here," he draws a slightly larger wedge nestled up to the first, "is what we don't know"–"DK." "The rest," he says triumphantly, scribbling through the vast expanse of pie, "is what we don't know we don't know"–"DKDK." Why on Earth, Avi wonders, would we spend all of our time in the smallest piece of the pie? The territory of DKDK beckons. Welcome to Avi's World.

Avi believes that our teaching identities must match up with our fuller life identities or we risk communicating that school matters in only one sense–getting to college, getting a good job–but not at all in other ways, for example, in the important business of figuring out who one is and what his or her life means. He quotes the 13th-century mystical poet, Rumi:

> There are two kinds of intelligence: One acquired,
> as a child in school memorizes facts and concepts
> from books and from what the teacher says,
> collecting information from the traditional sciences
> as well as from the new sciences.
>
> With such intelligence you rise in the world.
> You get ranked ahead or behind others
> in regard to your competence in retaining
> information. You stroll with this intelligence
> in and out of fields of knowledge, getting always more
> marks on your preserving tablets.
>
> There is another kind of tablet, one
> already completed and preserved inside you.
> A spring overflowing its springbox. A freshness
> in the center of the chest. This other intelligence
> does not turn yellow or stagnate. It's fluid,
> and it doesn't move from outside to inside
> through the conduits of plumbing-learning.
>
> This second knowing is a fountainhead
> from within you, moving out.

Avi adds, "I wish we could teach from this place of intuition, passion, the right-brain thinking. I wish this kind of talk wouldn't elicit derisive laughter among my colleagues."

Race, gender, love, death, sexuality, drugs, pleasure, pain, disease—these are all regular topics of discussion in Avi's World. "We're a pretty sophisticated group," Avi says. The second kind of tablet summons us, "and we don't shy away from much." In fact, the whole question of boundaries, of what should and shouldn't be a part of class, is a regular discussion. Everyone agrees that Mr. Lessing's love life must remain off-limits.

"But in my experience," Avi continues, "issues play out in the room—up-close, personal—with an urgency that can't be faked or manufactured or imposed from the outside." Since this is America at the beginning of the 21st century, first and foremost is the issue of race. Students can talk easily about the ins and outs of race matters: race as a social construction, race as a hierarchy of privilege and oppression, race as both material and ephemeral, both the most fantastic American illusion and the harshest and most costly American reality.

One White student was presenting a story in class about ice skating, and she noted in passing that most African Americans don't skate. A door began to yawn open—the categorical statement, the conclusional gesture—but she seemed oblivious, and so did Avi. She speculated on causation—the cold, the cost of skates—repeated a joke from Chris Rock or Dave Chappelle, she didn't remember, annotating her own hipness, and moved on.

When she finished, the conversation that followed percolated at a comfortably moderate temperature until an African American girl spoke up, steaming, and said that the comments about the expense of ice skates was just plain racist. Several students ignited suddenly and jumped forward to disagree. The African American girl stood her ground: "There are racist people in here," she said. And then the storyteller burst into tears and left the room, followed by half a dozen students eager to support her in her distress. The African American girl, her face tight, was unyielding: "You see that? That's what I mean: She makes a racist comment, and no one races over to comfort me. Now she's got to be taken care of, and here I am."

White privilege is a hidden curriculum everywhere, but in Avi's World, it's assumed to be a point of interrogation and question-asking. Avi doesn't buy into the common sense of racial innocence or the logics of privilege: color blindness, avoidance, white-washing. Here, the choice appears to be racial responsibility or racial irresponsibility. Avi wants everyone in class, including himself, to choose the rocky road of honesty and responsibility.

Earlier in the year, on the first day of theater class, Avi told a group of African American boys wearing starter jackets to quiet down. They didn't and so he raised his voice: "You guys!" One student responded, "What do you mean, *you guys?*" What did he mean? He wondered. Here, he was directing "Twilight" by Anna Deavere Smith, with its opening monologue asking the provocative question, "Who's *they?*", and he'd essentially labeled these three kids. But weren't they disturbing the class? Hadn't he merely tried to get order? That rationalization blanketed an implicit assumption, however, that he'd made prior to class even beginning. "In truth," Avi says now,

> I came in with the expectation that those three students, the darkest and most typically male, the biggest in size, would be trouble. They had walked in the room, and I had shrunk back. That realization carries some shame for me even now, but it was also an open door to walk in. If I couldn't see those boys properly, how could I teach them? And how much had their experiences been shaped by other adults who, in one way or another, also shrunk back, and thought, *here comes trouble?*

He didn't have to look outside of the school for racism; it was right there, smack dab in the middle of things. "The next day, I apologized to those boys in front of the whole class." That didn't completely clear things up, and initially everyone felt a little uncomfortable. One student described the moment as the time when Avi "asked us to lean into our discomfort. . . . [I]t's like we're used to being hard in the world, but he wants us to be soft in this classroom, and so the rules out there don't apply here."

Avi's vision of a perfect school is a place where teachers get to be human beings, students get to see teachers make errors, be sad, even go grocery shopping, without surprise or shock or embarrassment. A bad school is where teachers behave like automatons, or, worse, classroom managers (which, to Avi, sounds like something out of Orwell) who dispense information to students:

> We're inundated with information, but starving for experience. We ought to be able to be real human beings not in despite of our work, but because our work demands it. What students most need—our humanness, our own moral dilemmas, our very real struggles, we somehow feel obligated to deny the opportunity to share. It is an untellable loss to the students and teachers.

"For me," Avi says now,

> all teaching has to start with the personal—even something that some
> would construct as impersonal, something like teaching math—because
> teaching always involves a human being engaged with other human
> beings, and the interesting thing is what happens to that teacher, to
> those students, and what happens in the field between them.

Avi thinks we all benefit, teachers and students alike, when we ask ourselves: Who are we? What are we doing here? What is any of this good
for? How are we feeling? What events, experiences, and memories trigger
which responses? Avi believes that teachers need to access the vertical and
the horizontal, the three-dimensional and the four-dimensional, the surface
and the deep.

"Numbness scares me," Avi says, "and death scares me." He wrote his
college thesis on the fear of death, and entitled it "So That I May Go On."
The thesis included the deaths of two friends——one in an auto accident,
the other from cancer—and remembered stories of the Holocaust in Europe
from his father. All life is suffering, he concluded, and loss. "But wisdom," he
now says, "comes from looking squarely into the fragility of it." He doesn't
shy away from the terrible because he thinks that it's only there that we can
learn to appreciate the good, the beautiful, and the just.

"Working on myself as a human being and working on my teaching are
not separate events," he says. Most schools, of course, divide these into two
distinct universes: Life and Job. "To me," he continues, "we can only know
our work to the extent that we know ourselves; and consciousness about
our work is also necessarily self-consciousness."

Avi does not let himself off the hook. He questions himself more sharply
than the students:

> This kind of self-discovery, or self-admitting of my own ineptitude, fear,
> and doubt about teaching became a powerful tool for me, acknowledging
> that I did not have to have all of the answers was far more useful
> than pretending that I did. Despite all of my intentions to do good in
> the classroom, there was a great possibility for doing harm, and that
> possibility increased when I made assumptions about who students
> were, and the ways they should act toward me. The possibility for
> misunderstanding increased when I taught students with backgrounds
> that were different from my own. I undoubtedly connected more

easily to Jewish students that, like myself, grew up upper-middle-class; however, most of my students did not fit that narrow description. And yet, I realized early on that I saw color, and if people said they did not, I was suspicious of them. How do you not see color with the history of our country, with the present predicament of our cities, of the way our schools are de facto segregated? How can teachers and students cross the real divides that separate us?

Avi is a mildly polarizing character, someone sketchy to some and honored by others in the same space and sometimes in the same breath. Almost no one is neutral on Avi. Maya, who loves his class, says, "No one listens to us like Mr. Lessing; he looks at you and his *eyes* are listening." Another student tells him at the end of the term that he didn't teach anything at all, and "You just pick a few books *you* like and that's not teaching. Where's the English?" Nonetheless, Avi's class is the hangout spot at lunch and free periods for a large crowd of kids, and not just the ones with sandals and turtlenecks.

"I'd like to be closer to my colleagues," he says. "I got into teaching because it was a place I could bring my whole self." He'd hoped to find many, many others who felt that way—he was hired even after telling the chair that he had no interest in teaching reading and writing—but it's been hard. "I led a long meditation in a department meeting when I was first here," he says, "and that turned out to be miscalibrated and pretty divisive." A few people like it, most found it odd and eccentric, and for a few it was reason to distrust him ever after. "To me learning *stuff* is the easy part, and yet that's all that our schools obsess about; thinking is tough, feeling is tough, and that's what I'm interested in." Schools say: *Don't teach the personal*; Avi says: *Take it all personally*. That focus on teaching the taboo makes him a weirdo, an outlaw, and a hero.

Avi is not alone, of course, even when he feels lonely, nor is he unique. There are Avi's Worlds all over the country. These are the creative spaces where we can create our lives, the honest places where the truth is told, the safe havens where a person can breathe in the good air and breathe out the bad air, where the real stuff is on display and not suppressed. Jeff Kass in Ann Arbor; Katie Hogan, Dave Stovall, and Erica Meiners in Chicago; Marc Bamuthi Joseph and Wayne Yang in the Bay Area; and Yvonne Smith in New York—these teachers just keep showing up.

Things move on, of course, and people change. Avi is a kind of fixture on the third floor now, and there are small gestures and little victories: An art teacher approached Avi about collaborating on teaching a documentary next year, and a custodian who attended a performance of a class play told him, "Now I see what you're doing with these kids. Nice work."

One morning, a 17-year-old girl, blond, small, her eyes red and swollen, took the floor. "I'm pregnant," she said in a whisper and then began choking back sobs. The class reeled, caught its collective breath, as several students came to her side to hold her hands or rub her shoulders. She hadn't told her parents, only the father of the baby—who was also, remarkably, present in the class, squirming a bit but trying to hold up—and her closest friends. But today she was spotting heavily, and she planned to tell her mom right after school. How did it happen? Should she get an abortion? Was the boy committed to her? What were her choices and her chances? Avi intervened rarely, but always as the grownup, and here he took charge: Telling your mother is best for you; you should see a doctor today. For an hour, there was an emotional intensity and intellectual engagement rarely seen in high school. As class ended, everyone agreed to shut up about it until she could tell her mom, and then students lined up to hug her, many to cry with her.

After class Avi called his mother, a therapist—he's still young enough. He felt a little despairing and he asked her if she thought he belonged in a school, if his teaching had any value whatsoever. "You belong there," she assured him, "because you're still able to ask that question." That reminded him of something one of his teachers used to ask in all kinds of fraught and complex situations: Is that the dharma you've heard or the dharma you've experienced?

The noise of the day subsided and he felt better. This was the dharma of his own experience. This was Avi's World.

FOUR.

Tell No Lies:
Science and Math Matters

In order to attain knowledge, which is a form of power, we cannot continue to endorse, with blinded vision and stilted jargon, the initiation rituals with which our spiritual high priests seek to legitimize and protect their exclusive privileges of thought and expression. . . . We do not want to be like the scientist who takes his umbrella with him to go study the rain.

—Ariel Dorfman and Armand Mattelart, *How to Read Donald Duck*

"I hate science and I hate Mr. Korshak." Demaine, 16, sharp in conversation and sharp in analysis, consistently received grades that failed to reflect his smarts. Sometimes teachers defined him as lazy; sometimes "resistant." Demaine was difficult, no doubt about it.

When the grades came out for the first semester of Advanced Biology for the sophomore class, everyone was in shock: 20% were getting an F. These students had been part of an integrated class in a new small school within Barrie High School, one that brought all skill levels into the same classroom. The idea powering this move was a belief that detracking the kids, allowing everyone to work together, would simply result in everyone doing better. It was a rather naive notion, perhaps, but it was based on a hopeful if incomplete plan. A friendly and engaging young science teacher, Don Korshak, hadn't raised any red flags, hadn't given a warning, and now this.

The standard next step would be for this 20% to be dropped from Advanced Biology for the second semester, and put into Biology 1, a course not approved for California college admissions. This is the general practice of the science department and those who had not self-selected for Bio 1 from the start would be placed there by the spring, leaving the "better" students to carry on without the distraction of the weak or the unworthy.

This was a moment of crisis for these small-school teachers. The innovative program they had committed themselves to building was created around a cluster of classes—English, history, and a video elective—that could, they hoped, help develop a sense of community and support. But too many students were failing in their other classes—math, science, and language. To grow the program, teachers would need to offer the full range of classes, and find a way to be successful in every one.

The 20% failure rate triggered a series of difficult meetings and discussions that included staff, students, and their families. Arthur, Demaine's father, asked, "You mean you didn't notice this coming? Don't you check in with your new teachers? It may be your mistake but my son is paying for it. The promises the small school had made suggested they would do better than the factory-model school. But it was clear that the achievement gap would not be addressed unless we were fiercely committed to the hard work of unpacking the problems and finding solutions.

The teachers made a radical proposal to Korshak and the science department: "Don't drop any kids from the second semester of biology; let us teach a backup course after school 3 days a week during which the students who failed could relearn the first-semester material; allow a series of quizzes or assessments to demonstrate what the students know; and change their first-semester grades if they demonstrate mastery of the first-semester material by May of spring semester." It would be called the Biology Mastery Project.

This caused some discomfort: Word might get around among the students that you could fail the first semester and get a second chance in an afterschool program. Some science teachers worried that it set an unfair precedent—some students had passed Advanced Biology with the instruction they got in the time they were given; why should others be given special treatment? For many of the science and math teachers, their subject is understood as a discrete set of settled facts, equitably explained and written on the board. And the students distinguish themselves either by working hard and understanding this information or by displaying a deficient character and slacking off. The issues of how to engage students, of teaching methods, of cultural mismatches, of social context—all these are so much hogwash, dubbed "granola teaching" not worthy of a rigorous science program. Still, for this one time, in this one experiment, the Biology Mastery Project was given tentative approval.

Everyone had talked about equity, about detracking, about helping all students succeed. Everyone repeated an article of faith: All kids can learn. But could they, and would they? One thing was clear. Detracking does not create good results automatically, any more than group projects work simply by dividing students into groups. Putting all the students in a traditionally taught Advanced Biology class had produced predictable failures and a reproduction of the achievement gap.

When the students gathered for the first Biology Mastery Project, they framed the problem the way teens often do, subjectively, as a relationship problem. They were angry at Korshak and said he must simply not like them. And yet mostly they were resigned—not surprised by their expected failure, not hopeful that there was any real solution. Parents and teachers wanted action: What was the backup plan? How would student progress be measured?

The Biology Mastery Project was led by a counselor who would preside and keep track of student issues, commitment, and buy-in, aided by an English teacher. Two seniors, whose participation in the project constituted their internship for senior seminar, signed on: Sade Bonilla came from a working-class Puerto Rican family and had become a major activist in school reform and in pushing the school to live up to its promises; Diego Kusnir was also an activist with a father who had been driven from Argentina during the "dirty war" and a mother from Mexico. Both students were strong in science and excited to be involved.

Things did not start well. Fifteen students who had failed were invited to join the effort, and 13 were willing to give the backup class a try. Of these, 3 were Latino, 1 was white, and 9 were African American. The other 2 couldn't afford to miss their jobs—another obvious if typically unstated problem in trying to achieve equity. In public schools, Advanced Placement classes are always surrounded by armies of private tutors lifting students through them. Working-class kids don't have those options.

Digging into the content of the course, the team began to see the way the curriculum was constructed. Although this was a biology course, the first two units were all on chemistry. Instead of interesting students with exploration of systems and classification, of the workings of nature, modern biology curriculum relies on an "input model"—meaning is made through the construction of a pyramid of knowledge. Chemistry is the basis for much of biological calculation, so students who have never taken chemistry are given a cram course in the beginning of the year. But there was no time to question and reconstruct the setup of the course. The clock was ticking and they had to get through these units.

The first task was to understand the Bohr diagram of the atom and the characteristics of different elements as they appear on the Periodic Chart. Class started with chalk drawings, then manipulatives such as pipe cleaners and beads. This moved along pretty well. At the Lewis diagrams and bonding, things bogged down. Chemical reactions occur when atoms share or exchange electrons. Now they were into problems of an atom giving up an electron to another, creating positive and negative ions, or atoms sharing a pair of electrons, which is represented by two dots or a single line between the atoms. There were no problems with the actual interaction of the atoms when they took the time to draw it out and see what might happen. They used groups of people, kind of like a square-dance formation, with outer electrons doing a do-si-do.

The counselor started every session with a circle. Students shared how they were doing, what they hoped to accomplish that day, and an emotional temperature gauge. This was followed by the work plan for the day, with the overview delivered by Sade or Diego, and every adult acting as a tutor.

When the going got tough, some started to zone out, space out, drop out. Parents started coming to the after-school class, bringing snacks and checking that their kids were showing up. One day, Christina was tearing through some problem sets, since it was finally working for her, and Jasmine shouted at her, "What the hell are you doing? How are you getting that?" Tashelle started to cry, "We're finished. We'll never get this." Demaine moved to another table, asking Diego to help him walk through the steps of figuring out a series of bonds. Through tears, cajoling, joking, and sweating, the class geared up for its first quiz.

The quiz was a bust: Of the 13 students, only 4 had passed. Four. What was going on? What had gone wrong? What did the kids not get? The students were angry, charging that the quiz was unfair. It was confusing, they said, how the questions were written, how things were asked. Sade broke in: "I think you understand this stuff. The problem is that you're having trouble understanding what the quiz is asking you to do." Yes, they agreed. That night, she went home and wrote up a long critique of the quiz with proposed alternate ways of setting out the questions.

In place of questions such as, "What is the difference between the total number of electrons and the valence electrons? How is an ionic bond constructed? What is the reason that some atoms must form an ionic bond? How are the electrons organized?" Sade proposed:

Draw the complete Bohr model (the nucleus and each of the shells) for each of the four atoms listed. Also write down the number of protons, number of electrons, and number of electrons in the valence shell. Then show how the atoms would come together to form a compound. Draw a Lewis diagram of each compound, only showing the valence shells. Then name the chemical formula and chemical name to the best of your ability.

Much of the problem with the quiz was in the language, the way the problems were stated, the vague directions, what she described as "obscure" wording and confusing grammar. Sade's wording made everything more concrete, more like the practice work the students had been doing. So often, the problem teachers have arises from their idiom, their linguistic shortcuts and codes, which may work for some kids but are a foreign tongue for others. It is the discourse practices, the hidden codes of language reflecting White middle-class teachers, that create a longer journey for African American, Chicano-Latino, and immigrant students. Robert Moses argues that learning math and learning science is the same; it is a matter of learning another language. And if there are language mismatches already between the teacher and the student, this introduction of a new language is all the more confusing.

After 1 more week of review, extensive pep talks, and one long group meeting, the students took the quiz again. In fact, the new quiz was created by Sade and was twice as long as the first one and demanded more understanding. This time, all but one student passed. Not only that, but 10 of the 13 were doing quite well in the second semester of Advanced Biology where, curiously, the curriculum was set up so that more user-friendly subjects such as ecosystems were explored.

After the pain and difficulty of the first unit, things moved much faster. The students worked their way into a process of group study, so that it was not just adults and seniors doing the tutoring—it was now students teaching students. And by May, 9 of the 13 students had brought their first-semester grade up to a C, 3 had gotten to a B, and 1 had a D. There were hugs, laughter, high-fives, and even some tears on that day. Demaine and Jasmine perked up. Instead of reluctant, angry students, they became teachers. "This isn't so hard, really," bragged Demaine, with one big, infectious smile.

But the very success of the Biology Mastery Program has to give one pause. So this is what the achievement gap was all about? Three months. We have these kids locked down for 12 years in school and we could not give them 3 months to help them succeed? Are we really in that much of a hurry? Is this just another tool to construct difference, to create winners and losers? One thing was clear: If we have an achievement gap, we can be pretty sure it won't change if we don't do some things in fundamentally different ways.

Most of the students who were lost did not have problems with fundamental intelligence or even with scientific thinking. They were defined as behavior problems, bored or unengaged kids, attitude cases—the usual list of maladies. But what they were not getting was heard; what they were lacking was connection. Schools are guilty of constructing a connection gap—certainly across race and class borders, but also in relation to gendered identity. Proper science is defined as abstract, rational, and freakishly alpha male. There is no room for heart, intuition, or playfulness. In addition, the wisdom of indigenous cultures, of other pathways besides the Western one, are not welcomed into the discourse.

Just as education authorities in the United States create a kind of "school-writing" (the five-paragraph essay) that is stilted, uninspired, and unlike any writing you are likely to find in the real world, they also foist on us a kind of "school-science," a set of settled truths, of autonomous facts, algorithms, and worldviews that take the joy and adventure out of science. Not only is it boring, but it robs the discipline of its creative, changing, and beautiful core. Science class should be more like art—a field that values mistakes and false steps rather than the right answer.

Frank Oppenheimer, the radical physicist who founded the Exploratorium in San Francisco, had a vision of science as a matter of exploration, discovery, and playfulness. Students should not be bored; they should be astounded. "It shouldn't be pretty and under glass," he said. "The visitor should learn that experiments break, and fail, and you've got to fix it. Shops should be part of the museum. Because that is the way that physics is done. Things break. You fix them. You repair them. You change them. You improve them."[36]

When students began to teach one another, to rely on older students who are just 2 years ahead of them, to feel ownership of the Mastery Class space, they succeeded. More testing, more punishment, would not help students become better. This could only happen in the workshop space, a classroom that had to be approached with an open heart, uncertain as to what would work and unfettered by received wisdom about biology and about the capacity of these students.

These kids, almost all the students, got through this, through the crisis of it. But this was without really questioning the way the material was organized, without examining deeper questions. Did it have to be like this?

On another day, look in on a class of math and science undergraduates at a major university who are planning to become teachers, a group with strong representation of African American, Chicano-Latino, and first-generation immigrant students who are doing field placements as tutors and teachers' assistants in the public schools. When asked how many of them had family members who objected strenuously when they announced that they were going into teaching, almost every hand went up. Why did these students go against expectations? It often has to do with their desire to help kids, or to share a passion with kids, and as often it has to do with a teacher in their lives, someone who made a difference, who connected with them. They want to be that person for others.

But they feel intense frustration in those field placements, too. Here are university students who have made it through the Darwinian obstacle race that is U.S. math and science education, who have survived freshman year at a university where as many as 30% of science and math majors are pushed out of the field. They know how to suck it up and do what they are told. They are willing to memorize formulas and algorithms. Now they are back in schools like the ones they attended, and several report spotting almost immediately a student who represents themselves only a short time ago—the one who is going to fight her way through and make it. What about the others—the vast majority of students, really—who are destined to fail or run away from math and science as soon and as far as they can? Is there no way to speak to them? Can't we have a commitment to math and science literacy, and some enthusiasm to boot, which is the right of all citizens?

As we dig in to these questions, more fundamental ones come to the fore. We came to believe that math and science do not have to be taught this way, with a one-note delivery, an input model of logical progression of a set body of knowledge. Soon, however, we even began to wonder why these disciplines are constructed in such flat and closed-minded ways.

Sometimes it seems that many who have gone into science and math have been drawn to those fields because of the comforting sense of certainty, of a clear answer, of a lack of ambiguity. If this outlook dominates science and math education, it's unlikely to inspire the most important, even the most authentic, approaches.

Certainly, the processes of inquiry, of positing a thesis, of seeking evidence, of making an argument, all represent powerful experiences. In the West, these methods were developed in defiance of church dogma as part of the Enlightenment revolution. But effective, authentic science education would also engage the curiosity and creativity of students. Science is not a firm set of certainties—each step always ends with an open-ended question:

What next? What else? Why does it matter? Too often, science has been taught as the settled common sense of an era, something flat and formidable.

But accepted science turns out to be incorrect, or at least incomplete, quite often. Besides looking at the persecution of Galileo, we can go back a much shorter time: The pseudo-science of eugenics was perpetrated in the early 20th century by the great lights of the Progressive Era. In their social improvement project, these scientists applied a distortion of Darwinian method to suggest that there are lower and higher humans and that, indeed, social policy should seek to limit the births of African Americans and others deemed unworthy while cultivating the ascendancy of the "better types." Eugenics was used not only to perpetrate separate and unequal institutions in the United States, but it was adopted in Germany as the justification for racial policies, the extermination of disabled people, and ultimately, the Holocaust.

On the one hand, we can look at the ongoing process in science of one theory holding up for a while and then being supplanted, overcome, by a new and better series of observations and theories. In this sense, the most productive sense, science is always evolving. But the authoritarian construction of science broaches no challenge, defends its current iteration as the best and only truth. This is the flattening of science that keeps students out of the give-and-take, the lively process that represents the best in science.

On the other hand, we have plenty of cases of "bad" science, conclusions reached without any justification, which only had a grip on reality because of the social power of those proposing it. This would be the case of "cold fusion" in the late 1980s, or the case of data faking at Bell Labs in the mid-1990s. More recently, we can look at Nobel laureates in economics, whose complex metrics claimed to show how to value derivatives—supporting the creation of the crazy bubble that took down Wall Street in 2008. Now most agree that it was bogus science, a process that seemed to work only in an expanding economy.

This suggests that science requires a more inclusive community of people who are allowed to comment on and interpret the field—in other words, a more democratic science education that would make the engagement with current scientific discussions and debates an aspect of normal citizenship. It would be better for all of us if we created more of a dialogue, more of a community process to handle our society's interpretation of nature. Ironically, modern scientists have re-created the "religious" hording of knowledge that they so objected to in breaking from the medieval church-bound regime of knowledge.

And the voices of women, indigenous people, African American, Chicano-Latino, immigrant students, of all students, belong at the table. One of the rights that imperialist conquerors assumed for themselves was the right to name things, to define phenomena, to impose a kind of science that presupposed European and Western dominance, that subordinated other ways of seeing.

During the 1940s and '50s, physics in the West was elevated as the preeminent field because mankind was on a binge of invention and innovation—from rockets to nuclear energy and weapons. Our approach to physics was as a field that we could manipulate, control, and profit from. Biology, on the other hand, was seen as mostly a field for observation, to understand complex systems. Only in the last decade or so have the political and economic powers elevated biology, gambling that with genetic engineering we can construct the next great conquest of nature, the next economic bubble. The Western fetishism for finding a "key," a secret that unlocks the field, is typical of the American utilitarian drive to find a way to make a buck from any innovation. The Rockefeller Foundation was particularly eager to identify that key in biology and fiercely promoted DNA is the secret code of life. The campaign for DNA suggested that this was the answer to life and the road to riches, if we could only control and manipulate it. The real way that life, and growth, exists in a complex organism and within a complex environment is shoved aside in pursuit of profit and power.

This way of construing science, as feminist critics such as Madeleine Grumet, Sandra Harding, and Donna Haraway have pointed out, fits with the Western notion of a war against nature, a need to conquer nature and bend it to our wills. From the Bible suggesting that mankind was placed here to have dominion over nature to the drive of the Enlightenment and the Industrial Revolution, from the conquest of the Third World and the bending of all resources to the system of profit, nature has been seen as something for humans to manipulate and master. Even within our own psyche, Freud proposed that the id, our "animal nature," our drives, must be suppressed by the civilizing hand, the stern father, of the ego. Setting up this binary creates a worldview, a hierarchy, that privileges disembodied rationality over creativity, logic over intuition, and the master narrative over the vernacular voice.

All of these issues in science require deep engagement, political and ethical sensitivity, and debate. However, the way our schools teach science, disguising it as a neutral technology, seeks to divorce those who practice science from these very issues. Worse than that, it channels those who will be technologists of the system and those who will be leading scientists up the escalator of success while leaving the vast majority bored, alienated, and glad to finish science requirements as soon as possible.

A leading theoretical physicist, Freeman Dyson, argues that the best science is a human activity, not just a set of settled facts. It is an art form, not a philosophical method.

> Science is not governed by the rules of Western philosophy or Western methodology. Science is an alliance of free spirits in all cultures, rebelling against the local tyranny that each culture imposes on its children. Insofar as I am a scientist, my vision of the universe is not reductionist or anti-reductionist. I have no use for Western-isms of any kind. I feel myself a traveler on the "Immense Journey" of the paleontologist Loren Eiseley, a journey that is far longer than the history of nations and philosophies, longer even than the history of our species. . . . I was lucky to be introduced to science at school as a subversive activity of the younger boys. We organized the Science Society as an act of rebellion against compulsory Latin and compulsory football. We should try to introduce our children to science today as a rebellion against poverty and ugliness and militarism and economic injustice.[37]

Indeed, many of us are only now coming to appreciate the importance of indigenous knowledge, indigenous science, if you will, in relation to complex systems. The Incas did a much better job than the Irish and British in cultivating potatoes, maintaining diversity as a protection against devastating disease. The so-called Green Revolution in agriculture turned out to be an oil revolution—an energy-intensive, market-tied development that forced the dependence of local farmers on the Western corporations.

A key to understanding what we call science is the realization that all of these linked and disparate fields are at work within social contexts and social struggles. If Europe's "discovery" of new lands challenged everything they assumed about the universe and impelled scientific reinscription of reality, so the upheavals of the 1960s, the undermining of the master narrative of the great White Western man, transformed the scientific narrative.

For example, Thomas Kuhn wrote *The Structure of Scientific Revolutions* in the 1960s—debunking the great man theory of scientific breakthroughs. He demonstrated how an accumulation of insights, experiments, and challenges led up to each transformative theory. In other words, it was science from below, science from the social context. In the liberationist period of the 1960s, New Journalism dethroned the great man of the authoritative, neutral journalist in favor of the embodied, flawed, storyteller on the ground;

oral history suggested that history is not made by statesmen and generals but rather by the experiences, struggles, and solidarity of people on the ground. John Keegan revolutionized military history with *The Face of Battle*, which told the stories of key military engagements from the perspective of the common soldier and civilian, drawing startling conclusions.

Dyson argues, however, that science is neither an isolated intellectual conversation, driven by internal logic and observation, nor solely the product of social forces. Dyson says:

> Since I believe that scientists should be artists and rebels, obeying their own instincts rather than social demands or philosophical principles, I do not fully agree with either view of history.
> . . . The great advances in science usually result from new tools rather than from new doctrines. . . . Science flourishes best when it uses freely all the tools at hand, unconstrained by preconceived notions of what science ought to be. Every time we introduce a new tool, it always leads to new and unexpected discoveries, because *Nature's imagination is richer than ours.*[38]

So, although we must take into account the social context, the economics and politics of the day, these are not straitjackets within which one operates. After all, it took flights of imagination for the romantics to argue that the poor did not deserve their fate, that slavery was unnatural and criminal. They lived within their time and yet fought to transcend it, always in the direction of liberation, of richer and more fully realized lives. What can we do, as intellectual workers, as scientists, to embrace the artistic, the celebratory, the revolutionary aspects of science today?

Good teaching unsettles the questions and invites authentic inquiry. Powerful science and math education does not divorce numerical processes from the social context within which they live. Deep learning happens when students work together to solve problems, often inventing the processes or rules necessary to solve the problems.

The math program developed by Steve Rasmussen at Key Curriculum Press in Berkeley doesn't follow a straightforward progression of disciplines from arithmetic to algebra to geometry to trigonometry. Students may find themselves using ideas and skills from every aspect of math in addressing relevant problems that are posed in the curriculum. Students work out complex problems in groups, learning to communicate questions and to rely on one another to puzzle out possible solutions. Such a curriculum not only keeps a wide range of students engaged in math, it also teaches math concepts more deeply so students are not cramming for the test and then forgetting everything the next day. This is not to say that repetition and drill have no place in math—just as it does in becoming proficient at music, art, and sports. But a key aspect of music, art, and sports education is the development of a group culture around that skill, with a student mentored by a teacher or peer who knows them individually, in a situation that allows students to connect with others working on the same skill so that they can share triumphs, questions, and insights.

One difficulty is that in a problem-posing classroom, the teacher must be able to join a group of students that's gotten stuck, and understand whatever concepts the students used to get to the dead end. A weak math teacher, one who can drone out solutions on the board and grade tests, will often get lost in this messy process. And, as often happens with powerful innovations in curriculum, problem-posing math is often marginalized in high school by the parents of privilege, those who don't recognize the progression they remember from their own days and who want to see that calculus capstone at the top of their kid's transcript.

But, just as in science, we can question many of the received truths in math. For instance, why does calculus occupy the place of honor in mathematics, the top high school class that demonstrates academic success? Very few calculus students can even explain what it is for, just that it is "hella hard." Indeed, calculus is mostly useful in relation to physics, to evaluating changes over time. It is a matter of integration (the area under a curve) and differentiation (the slope of a curve). But it is of little use to most citizens, even most college graduates. Statistics would be a much more crucial cap class in math—one that is relevant to almost all fields and vocations, one that helps citizens evaluate research and the claims of experts. But stat is considered the easy way out, the less "challenging" option. Why? Who made it that way? Couldn't those who desire a science major in college pursue calculus, a kind of "mathematics of physics"? For that matter, why is physics set at the top of the hierarchy, a difficult and obtuse science class? Physics could be a fantastic 9th-grade class, one that is engaging and important—dealing from everything from fixing things to light and sound waves in music videos to speculation on the big bang. How did our sciences become so remote and forbidding?

Teachers have to learn to be creative, engaged, and experimental in order to be successful with all students. And if their language, teaching style, jokes, and ways of motivating don't work with students, it's the teachers who must challenge themselves to be successful. Some math teachers fail 40%, 60%, 80% of their students without batting an eye. But the truth is that, yes, even calculus can be exciting. Infinitesimals are interesting. But we must approach these subjects with the joy and immediacy that they deserve.

In our society, of course, science is the top legitimate body of knowledge. The social sciences suffer physics envy. Is it scientific? Does our work rise to the level of science? In educational research, quantitative research, anything with a number assigned to it, always gets more traction, more legitimacy. Many school administrators like to say they are "data-driven" even if the data are faulty, ridiculous, or stupid. If it has data, it must be good.

In a qualitative research class for graduate students, one that focused on ethnographic observation, the professor asked, "How can we show that qualitative research is scientific?" Being scientific stood as the key requirement, the sign that it was true. Would anyone ask, "How can we show that qualitative research is poetic?" "How does it contribute to insight, knowledge, understanding, joy, recognition, justice, empathy?"

Kim Allen, a physicist and green business consultant, tells us, "The quest of science is to identify those truths that exist regardless of who observes them. This would be fine if acknowledged as such, but the common vocabulary goes much further, naming these observer-independent truths as 'The Truth,' and all other types of knowledge—those that do depend on the observer—as 'not really true.'" In a sense, she says, we lose in profound ways by divorcing our lived, embodied selves from inquiries about nature. "There is a psychological price paid for believing that one's personal experience is neither important nor fully true. Few scientists are aware of this psychological pain because it is obscured by the very habit of removing and censoring oneself from one's experience."[39]

Math and science have never, in thousands of years of human history, been taught the way they are now. And in 10 years, they will be taught in completely new ways. Instead of passively following received wisdom, we teachers might work to rescue these fields from demoralization and boredom. In history, we can create our own primary sources through oral history; in English, we can engage in meaningful reading and writing within and across communities; and in math and science, we can approach school as a site of fascination, exploration, and creativity.

FIVE.

Banned, Suppressed, Bound, and Gagged

In a slave-holding country like this, there can be no such thing as *liberal* education tolerated by the State; and those scholars . . . however learned they may be . . . contented under their tyrannies have received only a *servile* education.

—Henry David Thoreau

The legendary children's book author Maurice Sendak and the iconic comic book artist Art Spiegelman collaborated on a cartoon strip for the *New Yorker* magazine, in which the two are seen strolling in the woods outside Sendak's home in Connecticut chatting about art, its meaning, and its impact. Sendak dismisses the notion that there's any real difference between art made for children and art made for adults. He argues that art is art—the same for adults and children—but Spiegelman doesn't buy it. "I wanna protect my kids," he says. Sendak responds:

Art, you can't protect kids, they know everything. . . . People say to me, "Oh, Mr. Sendak, I wish I were in touch with my childhood self like you," as if it were all succulent and quaint, like Peter Pan. Childhood is cannibals and psychotics vomiting in your mouth! I say, "You are in touch, lady—you're mean to your kids, you treat your husband like shit, you lie, you're selfish . . . that is your childhood self." In reality, childhood is deep and rich. It's vital and mysterious and profound. I remember my own childhood vividly . . . I knew terrible things . . . but I knew I mustn't let adults know I knew . . . It would scare them.[40]

Schools routinely suppress or deny the experiences of young people—they know terrible things, but they mustn't let the adults know that they know, and the adults are living in deep denial. Student voices are silenced, their insights ignored, their feelings patronized, their integrity undone, and sometimes, especially in high schools, enormous energy and resources are expended in a project of enforced ignorance. Most everyone accommodates the daily indignities—being told when you're hungry or when you're angry, when you can go to the bathroom or when you can eat—and it doesn't take long before students note and accept (or resist) the *Alice in Wonderland* world of school. Kids see the hypocrisy of it all, but when they name it for what it is, rather than being rewarded for their insights, their truth-telling, and their courage, they are quieted, and if persistent, labeled misbehaving rebels and treated like alienated outcasts.

We have too often banned truth-telling and the fully passionate side of life from our classrooms in favor of formality and politeness, cool rationality and distance. This is in classical terms, the valorization of Apollo and the banishment of Eros. Offering Eros, the whole person, a desk in the center of the room respects students as actively intelligent and three-dimensional people, invites and welcomes parents, the community, and the whole wide-ranging capacities of youth. As teachers, we can gesture toward all there is to see; we can accept the multiple perspectives and the wisdom in the room, and offer even more (and often odd or unfamiliar) lenses. We must, then, ourselves be driven by Eros, aware of our own desires and drives, resistant to categories. We work to develop the courage to throw open every window and door within our reach, to throw off the lifeless, gray, unpleasant, and unerotic in our teaching, and in this domain of the strange, illuminate emotional richness and humanity, unexpected and overwhelming beauty. In order to keep curriculum alive and emergent, we must be goaded by our own unanswered questions, the need to choose ourselves as alive and awake in a mass of contradictions, and to be caught up in things. Education is coming into the conversation—inviting our students in, and in turn being allowed into that conversation by our students.

Everything students pursue passionately—in their own spaces—is locked out, *persona non grata*, in the classroom. Official knowledge is stultified, the Dionysian circle dance repressed, face-painting, fire-walking, and whooping entirely sacrificed in favor of the worksheet and the standardized test. It's a dangerous dance, to be sure, to take a step toward inviting our students into the classroom in their dynamic multidimensionality. But the payoff may be worth the risk: It suggests that adults could allow the caring, feeling, dreaming aspects of young lives some air and light and water to bloom. It asks us to support the insights, concerns, and questions that students raise. Listen to the music: filled with longing and loneliness, desire and bodies, and yes commitment and caring. Turn up the volume.

One of the great literary explorations of this struggle is found in *The Oresteia*, which is often read as Aeschylus's horrifying and cautionary tale of the dangers found in jealousy, revenge, and usurping one's role. Clytemnestra is generally seen, like Lady Macbeth later, as the evil one who defies women's proper place.

But in the hands of curious and engaged students, no such easy reading is possible. They see Agamemnon returning from the Trojan War—the archetype of man-glory violence—following 10 years of destruction and butchery. He had even slaughtered his own daughter to propitiate the sea gods and assure his men a safe trip to Troy.

A feminist reading insists that we think of Clytemnestra differently. She abhors Agamemnon's alpha-male war worship, his pernicious violence, and his domination. He arrives home, and she slays him, boom! She is hunted down for revenge by her own sons, and she calls forth the Furies, the Earth goddess spirits, to support her complaint against her husband. Clytemnestra is, inevitably, defeated but her struggle for mother-right, for the home and hearth, for justice is inscribed in the majesty of the tragedy.

Perhaps we should consider another lens, consider the culture of war as a consequence of the ascendance of patriarchy, the power of men, over the communal, tribal societies that preceded them. This transition is explored in myth in the story of Zeus and the Olympian gods overthrowing Gaia, mother-right, and the older Earth gods, the Furies who then become identified with irrational hatred and passion. And the struggle continues.

The project of child domination masking as child protection, the strict father ethic embraced by the authoritarian, does not make children safe. It makes them subject to the whims of autocratic adults, and it can get them hurt in a thousand ways. Too often, youth are deserted, not allowed to live their own childhoods fully because they are forced to service the unfulfilled desires of adults—whether it is their desire to write the script for their children or to dominate them. The public revelations of sexual abuse of children by priests and ministers points to centuries of abuse and rape and torture and murder built on a base of sexual repression and hatred of the body coupled with authoritarian male power. By welcoming Sendak's *Wild Things* into the classroom, we support student agency and strong identity.

Whenever the subject of sex comes up in the minds of school people, the impulse is to desperately invoke the forbidden: the danger, the disease, the horror, the ruin that lurks in the realm of sexuality. Adults push that theme so often that any glimmer of joy and pleasure must be claimed in opposition to the adult world. Teachers seldom find ways to give sex-positive messages, to declare that sex is wonderful, delightful, multifaceted, and often precious. Adults are caught in their own debate between ineffective abstinence arguments and an obsession with condoms. But there is much that young people will experience with sex that has nothing to do with condoms—matters of desire and emotion, values and choice, coercion, manipulation, transcendence, and more. This, rather than the birds and the bees, is the conversation we are reluctant—and yet somehow required—to have with kids. In sexuality, as in all of education, we start by listening to our students, and we invite all voices into the room.

A caring, communitarian curriculum welcomes conflicting points of view. It opens doors, invites action, and expands domain of meaning. It breaks with the everyday common sense, the passive acceptance of the way things are. It moves into different provinces of meaning with distinctive modes of attending to the world, altered relations between objective and subjective, arts, dreams, quixotic fantasies. Teachers and students confront every issue, class, gender, ethnicity, nationality, race, White privilege. Teachers might move then beyond passive empathy and work through our own feelings of unease, our own blindnesses. Teachers and students can always ask themselves painful questions that become antidotes to the fearful specters of indifference. Teachers can always transcend passive empathy and instead create their teaching identities through conscious action on the side of the child.

A couple of mischievous 9th graders recently distributed a zine, an anonymously authored and unauthorized underground paper they had written over the weekend, clandestinely throughout their high school. This was the latest in a series of zines that had appeared in the school over several months. But although the earlier papers had focused on off-color humor and adolescent putdowns of other students, this one targeted faculty and administration—a recognized taboo.

In a typically extravagant and overheated comment, one story offered the opinion that Mr. Johnson ought to "have his ass kicked" for repeatedly looking down the fronts of girls' shirts. This was apparently a step too far, for while the earlier papers went largely ignored by administrative staff and faculty, this one met swift and decisive action. Students were called into the central office one by one, interrogated, broken down, forced to tell what they knew about Max Darden, one of the authors of the underground newspaper. Words like *slander* and *defamation* and *libel* were bandied about. It didn't take long for the miscreants to be located and expelled from school. Max's school contacted the colleges to which he'd been accepted and reported his expulsion. All his college acceptances were rescinded. He spent the next 2 years working at a Blockbuster. Now, 10 years later, he has never gone to college and works as a bartender.

The message to everyone was clear: Don't mess with power. If you want to be silly and irreverent, insulting or mean, keep the mudslinging at your peer level; talk about teachers in a disparaging way—regardless of the truth—and you will pay a heavy price. Interestingly, no adult ever asked Mr. Johnson if he did, indeed, look down girls' shirts. That would break another sacred taboo, the importance of adult solidarity in the face of the threat of the potentially unruly mob.

Little wonder, then, that practically every high school in America is built on two separate and unequal cultures: an authorized, official adult culture, and a semi-secret, sometimes subversive youth culture. Interestingly, the adults, who often think they know the real story of what goes on in school, have only a partial, sketchy understanding that another and distinct culture even exists (except as cute slang words and unacceptable musical taste), while the kids tend to have a laser-like bead on the nuances, complexities, and parameters of the adult world. Come to think of it, Mr. Johnson probably *did* look down girls' shirts.

Of course, the powerless in every situation keep secret tabs on the powerful; they're like little ethnographers gathering, sorting, and theorizing data—they need to know where the next blow might be coming from. And although those in power have an intense interest in those beneath them on the pyramid, it's in the very nature of the relationship that, try as they will and even employing their greater experience, resources, access, and machinery, they simply can't see it and don't get it.

The real lives of young people peek out all the time, often to the horror of the adults, sometimes to their shame. Francois Truffaut's *The 400 Blows* recounts his own childhood, invoking the French saying that a child does not reach adulthood until he has been struck by an adult, often at school, 400 times. It is a story of abuse, yes, but also of his underworld resistance, his brilliant insights and meaning-making and invention of himself in opposition, his clandestine exercise of agency and dark humor. It becomes a testament to life.

Teachers who make a space of honest exploration and serious examination of the embodied lives gathered in classrooms offer their students the possibility of re-integration, re-creation, and re-affirmation in ways neither clandestine nor dangerous. Opening this window to the truth, classroom culture can begin to crackle and sizzle, and the environment can suddenly start to dazzle and glow.

Listening to students, taking their lives seriously as a point of departure, invites us to live alongside them in the eternal and never-ending search for happiness, reason, meaning-making, reverence, and hope. We want them to develop minds of their own, we want them to be able to name the world, we want them to link their own growing consciousness with their everyday conduct, and we want them to live lives that are arcing forward, infused with hope. This can never happen in the all-too-familiar constrained and strangled classrooms of pure authority, it can never come to life in the absence of Eros.

This is one sure way to help them resist superstition and fundamentalism, and to move beyond simple expressions of liberty and tolerance. We can't solve every problem in our classrooms, but we can create spaces where happiness is cherished, reason is respected, integrity and dignity are upheld and revered, and authentic hope a real possibility. This means highlighting the human capacity to notice or invent the possibilities for action. We can take as our standard the necessity of interrogating all that is before us, noticing what the real world is, of course, but also exploring what could be the case or what we might do to make a different case, and perhaps most important, what should be the case. We are not simply victims of our own lives, but also actors, creators, inventors, works-in-progress, and artists in residence.

In all of this, we strive to move beyond the simple-minded and one-dimensional narratives that dominate the public square. Among these we have a particular abhorrence for the wildly popular "victim narratives" that glorify as heroes those who have been hurt or harmed. We do not deny the common human experience of pain, loss, or unearned suffering. But we do see the victim-as-hero story in its endless repetition on "talk shows" and "reality TV" and the daily news as a denial of agency and human freedom, an obstacle to hope, and ultimately, then, an essentially immoral stance.

Zora Neale Hurston famously proclaimed, "I am not tragically colored. There is no great sorrow dammed up in my soul, nor lurking behind my eyes. I do not mind at all."[41] Making fun of the many well-wishers who seek a redemption project related to her disadvantage, who prefer to trap her in role of victim, needing the White man to rescue her, Hurston demanded her agency, her right to claim her identity and love it.

In a similar vein, Nikki Giovanni wrote in her poem "Nikki-Rosa,"

I really hope no white person ever has cause
to write about me
because they never understand
Black love is Black wealth and they'll
probably talk about my hard childhood
and never understand that
all the while I was quite happy[42]

Likewise, Eric Rofes, the late great teacher and education writer, insisted that he was never "tragically gay."[43] Even as a young student, he made choices that were subversive and important, and he does not want that courage, that insight that he so consciously invented, to be invalidated with the notion that he was merely a passive victim. Eric Rofes argued that he was a joyful practitioner of his queer identity, someone who had dared to break sexual rules and forge honest relationships based on authentic caring. Still, he demanded that he did not want entry into their society as it is—he sought to build a society in which he didn't have to seek entry. Rofes, like Maurice Sendak, dares to declare that students are whole, embodied humans—endowed with agency and dreams and, yes, with sexuality. We comfort ourselves by forgetting our own youth, by projecting onto youth a kind of blank and empty-minded innocence.

Teachers are not invited to do missionary work, charity work, among the oppressed in our society. Instead, we have an opportunity to be in the presence of tremendous, powerful, insightful young people. We can join in the dance with students and provoke them with questions, challenges, tools, and reflection, but we are only useful agents in their educations if we replace charity with solidarity, patronizing with respect. This requires a leveling of power in the classroom and a concerted search for generative topics, resources, and questions to pursue together.

SIX.

Queer the Common Sense

When a 16-year-old Indian immigrant girl named Chanti Kiran died in a
carbon monoxide leak at an apartment just a short walk from Berkeley
High School in November 1999, it was high school journalists who began
to question why she was not in school and who later learned, from other
South Asian students, about the practices of the multimillionaire landlord,
Lakireddy Reddy, of importing youth from India as indentured servants,
forced to work long hours in dangerous conditions, subject to every kind of
abuse and exploitation. Members of the regular press, with its teams of paid
reporters, had listed a short item about the death, but were not at all curious
about the back story. It was the identification of the kids with Chanti Kiran,
and their curiosity about her life and death, that pushed them to pursue the
story that led to Reddy's arrest and conviction.

But there was more. The national media jumped on the story—one of
those feeding frenzies. The students quickly found themselves losing control
of the story as it was bent to the national narrative. It went from a story of
culture clash and indentured servitude to an anti-immigrant sensation with
the evil kingpin in the middle; it morphed from a tale of abuse to a leering

story of "sex slave rings." The victim, instead of getting her respect as a person deprived of her rights and life, became the object of curiosity—the exoticized and eroticized South Asian female, with everyone clamoring for a photograph of her.

The students responded to some interview requests, and refused others. *Good Morning America* decided to cancel its planned coverage when the students would not go along with the sensational angle. One woman reporter who called and didn't get the story she'd expected yelled at the student editor-in-chief, "Do you know who you're talking to?" Another, a reporter from *Glamour* magazine, sent an e-mail to demand that the students drop what they were doing to provide her with a FedExed copy of the paper. She wrote:

> Personally, I would just as soon drop the story altogether. I'm on three other deadlines right now, and as you might imagine I have better things to do with my time than get into a pissing contest with uncooperative teenagers. . . . Most journalists in the real world cooperate with one another as a professional curtesy (*sic*) and because you never know—you might need the favor returned someday. . . . I apologize if your attitude has tarnished my view of the (student newspaper) and teenagers in general.

The students sighed, brushed it all off as the work of deluded adults, and continued with their newspaper work. The eyes of these reporters/students translate what is seen into a fine print every day. In their presence, we can preserve a record, an observed fragment of eternity.

"How is it," Edward Said asks, "that the premises on which Western support for Israel is based are still maintained even though the reality, the facts, cannot possibly bear these premises out?" In a notable 1984 essay, "Permission to Narrate," Said attempts to answer his own complex question: "Facts," he writes, "do not at all speak for themselves, but require a socially acceptable narrative to absorb, sustain, and circulate them."[44]

He's right, of course. Think, for example, of newspaper headlines you've seen that, while the facts and the content may be upsetting, are nonetheless instantly absorbed because they fit easily into a script already written—that is, they conform to a socially accepted narrative: "Toddler Left Unattended in South Side Apartment Bitten by Rat"; "Eight City High Schools Labeled 'Failing'"; "Two Teens Charged in Playground Shooting."

The facts in each of these situations are supported by a familiar and, therefore, comfortable story. The story absorbs the facts, sustains them, and circulates them repeatedly, far and wide. It often seems as if these stories are already written, resting comfortably in the back of a computer somewhere, awaiting only this or that predictable fact as authenticating detail, at which point they explode instantly onto the front pages.

Imagine the disequilibrium that would accompany a headline that organized the same set of facts in the service of a different narrative: "Failure of City to Eradicate Vermin Claims Another Victim"; or "City Bureaucracy Delays Child-Care Benefit; Unattended Boy Sustains Rat Bite"; "Chronic Underfunding of Urban Schools Reaps Predictable Results"; "Easy Access to Assault Weapons Puts Guns in Kids' Hands."

Or think of the site of ritualized hyper-narratives in conflict: the courtroom. From car accident to corporate looting, from criminal case to child custody dispute, the struggle is always a fight to fit the available facts for judge and jury into a credible narrative that serves a specific outcome.

At a trial we observed years ago, a large group of Irish Americans and recent Irish immigrants, all known supporters of the Irish Republican Army (IRA), had been charged in federal court in Brooklyn with accumulating weapons to send to the IRA in support of the struggle with Great Britain. The prosecution contended that the political beliefs of the defendants, along with their avowed support of the IRA, motivated them to conspire and break a number of federal statutes.

The defense told a different story: The defendants, they maintained, were part of a long and proud tradition of anti-colonial struggle against imperialist powers like Britain, a tradition that embraced the founding of the United States itself. Further, there was no criminal intent, since the defendants were convinced that they were acting in concert with U.S. policy and as adjuncts to a known federal agency.

Farfetched? Why? Which version is incredible?

It happens that the defendants in this case were acquitted. How? For one thing, the defense had an insight that the prosecution apparently missed entirely—they worked systematically to put an audience in the jury box that would be receptive to *their* narrative. The facts were only in minor dispute; the larger argument was over whose narrative to believe.

The defense succeeded in selecting a jury that was overwhelmingly made up of recent immigrants from Spanish-speaking countries, from Central and South America. The trial took place at the height of the Malvinas/Falklands crisis, an ugly war between England and Argentina that almost went nuclear. The crisis didn't register with most Americans, but it was a top story in Latin America, where the undisputed villain was Great Britain. For those jurors at that time, a narrative of independence from the evil empire was easy to hear, completely acceptable to believe.

Imagine if we took the headlines or the court cases not as narcotics to anesthetize ourselves against reality but as points of departure into real inquiry and authentic engagement.

This is the reason that young people make particularly powerful journalists—whether through their school paper, an underground paper, a Youth Radio segment, or a song or tag. It is not that they are amateur journalists or unformed journalists; they are, rather, journalists who are young and who bring their own perspectives. There are some things they may not see, but there are many other things that they *do* see, and see in fresh and startling ways.

We live in a world of perspective and point of view, of meaning-making and interpretation, of narration and storytelling. There is, of course, an objective world out there, but it's not a single, apprehensible world, flat and still and immutable, the same for all. People, objects, events simply never have a fixed, unchanging, or uncontested meaning. A slab of rock may be insignificant to one passerby, a milestone to the next, a boundary marker to someone else, and, in another context altogether, a piece of sculpture or a weapon. It all depends. And what it depends upon, plainly, is the construction and dissemination of meaning.

Nothing speaks for itself: People, restless and relentless meaning-makers that we are, invest meaning in things by how we use them, how we think and feel about them, how we act with and upon them, and how we story them. That slab of stone may become a foundation or a deck for a house; a pile of stones might become a house itself because of how we use it; that house may become a home because of how we come to feel about it, how we experience and describe it, the stories we tell about it; the whole becomes transported into a museum piece from an ancient civilization because of how we re-imagine it.

Every narrative is, of course, necessarily partial and incomplete, each a kind of translation or distortion. Reality is always messier, always more complicated and dynamic, always more idiosyncratic than any particular story can honestly contain. A single insistent narrative by its nature lies.

Perhaps that's why courtrooms are ultimately dissatisfying—sometimes profoundly, often mildly so: We tend to get a black-and-white world, a space where facts are altered and ignored; where messy, sensory reality is shunned; where illusions are the everyday currency blinding everyone to both large and small moral failings and inconvenient inconsistencies. One narrative must vanquish the other, one side must emerge crowing and triumphant and vindicated, while the other staggers away humiliated and beaten.

In newsrooms, too, there seems to be little room for nuance, none at all for two contradictory narratives existing side-by-side. Here's the story—beginning, middle, and end—neatly summed up in a single package, all the news that's fit to print.

When a single narrative takes on the authority of truth—when it puffs itself up to a size and a density that overshadows every contradiction or alternative possibility—it becomes like a magnetic hole in space, consuming all available energy and light, sucking the air out of every room. It deceives itself and works overtime to deceive everyone else, making a mockery of truth and a coherent moral universe in the process.

And perhaps that's what makes classrooms at their best such infinitely wondrous places: Not only can all the master narratives and triumphalist stories—as well as all manner of orthodoxy—be challenged and laid low, but whatever emerges in that process as the new truth, the new convention, can then be questioned, reflected upon, seen as inadequate in itself. Classrooms at their best can become the most natural and persistent sites of curiosity, investigation, skepticism, and agnosticism.

"Truman lied . . . Eisenhower lied . . . Kennedy lied . . . Johnson lied and lied and lied . . . Nixon lied . . . ," Daniel Ellsberg said, in the 1974 Academy Award–winning documentary *Hearts and Minds*, as he tried to explain domestic support for the American war against Vietnam. "The American public was lied to month by month by each of these five administrations. . . . It's a tribute to the American public that their leaders perceived that they had to be lied to." To sell a war there must be a threat—a manufactured threat will do—and there must also be a high-sounding purpose, even if the avowed purpose is, in fact, a lie.

The courageous journalist I. F. Stone had a simple rule of thumb that guided all of his efforts as a reporter, and he urged his colleagues to keep this at the center of their consciousness: Remember, he said, that all governments lie; the first task of journalists is to find out how and why. China and the old Soviet Union, of course, and now Russia, but also Algeria, Bulgaria, Cambodia, Dominica, Egypt, France, the Gambia—the entire alphabet of nations lies. And in spite of our hopes and aspirations and mystifications, the United States is no exception. In fact, the United States—near the bottom of the alphabet—is right up with the top-tier liars. Perhaps it's U.S. military power or economic reach, perhaps it's the sense of self-importance and destiny, but whatever drives it, our government lies to us and to the world from morning until night, from Sunday to Saturday, 24/7.

A brief history lesson then—read Howard Zinn! Read Howard Zinn!—should at least allow us to proceed as skeptics:

- President Polk cast Mexico as the aggressor in 1846, saying it had "Shed American blood upon the American soil"—a lie—and proceeded to seize half of that nation "in self-defense"
- President McKinley said in 1898 that the United States had a moral obligation to "liberate" the Cubans from Spain, and later to "civilize" the Filipinos—all lies—as he conquered new territory and murdered hundreds of thousands of patriots and resisters and ordinary people
- President Wilson prodded the country into World War I to "make the world safe for democracy"—a lie—as he joined the frenzy to divide the Earth and its resources and markets among the old and emerging imperial powers
- President Truman claimed that Hiroshima was a "military target"— a lie—and that dropping nuclear bombs on Japan saved "a million American lives"—an invention of monstrous proportions
- President Johnson lied about the Gulf of Tonkin, and before him Kennedy lied about the extent of U.S. entanglement in Vietnam, and after each of them, Nixon lied about expanding the war into neutral Cambodia

On and on and on—Ronald Reagan lied about Grenada; George Bush lied about Panama and Iraq; Bill Clinton lied about the Sudan; George W. Bush lied about weapons of mass destruction in Iraq and the extent of the Al Qaeda network; in 2010, as Afghanistan's puppet president visited the White House, he assured the administration that he was taking steps to curb corruption (a lie) and Barack Obama assured him of a long-term commitment (a lie). . . . It never ends. And all of it is promoted by a stenographic, lifeless press, and serviced by a bloated nationalist triumphalism, a distorted sense of collective self-worship, and a celebration of our inherent virtuousness and the nastiness of anyone who doesn't share that view.

And lying—not just by politicians and generals—is simply an expected and accepted, indeed, a central aspect of our social lives together. Imagine a world, for example, without "public relations" departments, spin doctors, or advertising agencies. We'd hardly know what to do; the landscape would be so foreign to us. We encounter thousands and thousands of ads every day from every direction. They're unavoidable, and many are clever, creative, and catchy. They are also—and everyone knows it—lies, lies set in motion to deceive, manipulate, bully, coerce, and undermine our confidence and integrity. And yet, even knowing the falseness of them, we sometimes marvel at their humor or artistry. Why? And how do we rationalize the value of everyday lying in public? How do we justify supporting a respected class of professional liars? What do we calculate this does to the soul of our culture or to truth-telling more generally? How do parents and teachers explain this to children who are clamoring to consume the next thing, and the next?

We are witnessing in public and political life a steady barrage of lying as justification for war, invasion, repression, torture, constant surveillance, and occupation. We are sold a terrifying scenario of risk, as well as a romanticized version of our beneficent mission in the world. Educators must ask ourselves if we are helping our students look critically at these and other received truths steadily raining down from the powerful. Are students able to separate fact from fancy? Can they interrogate whatever nonsense is given to them? Can they identify arguments and sort through conflicting claims and various sources of information in a steady and thoughtful and engaged way? Can they talk back? Can they imagine themselves acting effectively within the world?

Imagine a project of investigating the truth claims of advertisements.

Imagine kids interrogating the common sense all around them.

When military recruiters showed up at James Johnson High School in Chicago, a group of parents began to object, and one enterprising history teacher engaged his students in a curriculum of questioning:

- What questions do you have about the military?
- What purposes does the military serve?
- Why do military recruiters come to this school, but not the magnet schools or the schools in the wealthy suburbs?
- What kinds of recruiters do other kids in other schools get? Is it the same as our students get? Is it better? How about kids in other cities or other states or other countries?
- What role does the military play in our community, in the country, and in the world?
- Are there any alternatives to the military as a force for peace?
- Why are some youth attracted to the military?
- What are the working conditions in the military?

They found that in 2001 Chicago's mayor, Richard M. Daley, commented on an article in the online journal *Education Next* by then-mayor of Oakland, California, Jerry Brown. Brown's essay offered a rationale for the public military academies he was promoting for Oakland. In his letter to the editor, Daley congratulated Brown's efforts and explained his own reasons for creating military schools in Chicago:

We started these academies because of the success of our Junior Reserve Officers Training Corps (JROTC) program, the nation's largest. JROTC provides students with the order and discipline that is too often lacking at home. It teaches them time management, responsibility, goal setting, and teamwork, and it builds leadership and self-confidence.[45]

The students also discovered that Chicago has the most militarized public school system in the nation, with Cadet Corps for students in middle school, more than 10,000 students participating in JROTC programs, more than 1,000 students enrolled in one of the five, soon-to-be six, autonomous military high schools, and hundreds more attending one of the nine military high schools that are called "schools within a school." Chicago has a Marine Military Academy, a Naval Academy, three army high schools and an air force high school, making it the only city in the nation to have academies representing all branches of the military. And Chicago is not the only city moving in this direction: The public school systems of other urban centers with largely Black and immigrant low-income students, including Philadelphia, Atlanta, and Oakland, are being similarly re-formed—and deformed—through partnerships with the Department of Defense.

As military recruiters nationwide fall short of their enlistment goals—a trend spanning a decade—and as the number of African Americans enlistees (once a reliable and now an increasingly reluctant source of personnel) has dropped by 41% over the last several years, and the Department of Defense has partnered with the Department of Education and city governments both to sell its "brand" to young people and to secure positions of power over the lives of the most vulnerable youth. The federal No Child Left Behind Act is particularly aggressive, providing unprecedented military access to campuses and requiring schools to provide personal student information to the army. In many schools, JROTC programs replace physical education courses, recruiters assist in coaching athletic teams, and the military is provided space to offer kids a place to hang out and have a snack after school.

Chicago's Senn High School, which serves a working-class immigrant population—last year its students hailed from more than 60 countries—was forced, against the express wishes of the school and local community, to cede a wing of its building to a public military school.

Four core questions shaped a more formal inquiry, and while the investigation proliferated into scores and then hundreds, these became the basis of a report that the class issued and organized around.

1. Why has public education traditionally been a civilian, not a military, system?
Public education in a democracy aims broadly to prepare youth for full
participation in civil society so that they can make informed decisions about
their lives and the future of society as a whole. The Department of Defense
has a dramatically more constrained goal in our schools: influencing students to "choose" a military career. The military requires submissiveness
and lock-step acquiescence to authority, while a broad education for democratic living emphasizes curiosity, skepticism, diversity of opinion, investigation, initiative, courage to take an unpopular stand, and more. This dis-
tinction—of a civilian, not a militarized, public education system—is one for
which earlier generations fought.

During World War I, national debates took place over whether or not
to include "military training" in secondary schools. Dr. James Mackenzie,
a school director, argued, in a remarkably resonant piece published in the
New York Times in 1916: "If American boys lack discipline, by all means,
let us supply it, but not through a training whose avowed aim is human
slaughter."[46] In 1917, a report issued by the Department of the Interior
pointed out that "in no country in the world do educators regard military
instruction in the schools as a successful substitute for the well-established
systems of physical training and character building." And in 1945, high
school students in New York held public discussions about "universal military training" in schools, where some, an article noted, expressed "fears
that universal military training would indicate to the world that we had a
'chip on our shoulders.'"[47]

2. Are military programs in schools selectively targeted? Professor Pauline Lipman of the University of Illinois at Chicago has documented that Chicago's public military academies, along with other schools offering limited
educational choices, are located overwhelmingly in low-income communities of color, while schools with rich curricula, including magnet schools,
regional gifted centers, classical schools, IB programs and college prep
schools, are placed in whiter, wealthier communities, and in gentrifying
areas.[48] In other words, it's no accident that Senn High School was forced
to house a military school, while a nearby selective admission high school
was not. This is apparently a Defense Department strategy—target schools
where students are squeezed out of the most robust opportunities, given
fewer options, and perceived, then, as more likely to enlist; recruit the
most susceptible intensively, with false promises and tactics that include
bribes, gifts, home visits, mailings, harassment, free video games promot-

ing the glories of war and offering chances to "kill," and more. Indeed, the Defense Department spends as much as $2.6 billion each year on recruiting.

3. Are military schools and programs promoting obedience and conformity? Mayor Daley's claim that "[military programs] provide . . . students with the order and discipline that is too often lacking at home" taps into and fuels racialized perceptions and fears of unruly Black and Brown families and youth. They must be controlled, regulated, and made docile for their own good, and for ours. An authentic commitment to the futures of these kids would involve, for a start, offering exactly what the most privileged youngsters have: art education, including dance, music instruction, theater and performance, and the visual arts; sports and physical education; clubs and games and after-school opportunities; science and math labs; lower teacher-student ratios; smaller schools, and more. Instead, to take one important example, a recent study by the Illinois Arts Council reports that in the city of Chicago, arts programs are distributed in the same way as the other rich educational offerings—White, wealthy communities have them, while low-income communities of color have few or none.

A 16-year-old student attending the naval academy in Chicago said "When people see that we went to a military school, they know we're obedient, we follow directions, we're disciplined." She understood and accurately described the qualities that her school aims to develop—unquestioning rule-following.

4. Are military schools and programs promoting and practicing discrimination? Although the Chicago Board of Education, city of Chicago, Cook County, and the state of Illinois all prohibit discrimination based on sexual orientation, the U.S. military condones discrimination against lesbians, bisexuals, and gay men. Promoters of these schools and programs are willfully ignoring the fact that queer students attending these schools can't access military college benefits or employment possibilities, and that queer teachers can't be hired to serve as JROTC instructors in these schools. This double standard should not be tolerated. Following the courageous examples of San Francisco and Portland, Chicago could refuse to do business with organizations that discriminate against its citizens.

Military schools and programs depend on logics of racism, conquest, misogyny, and homophobia. Military schools need unruly youth of color to turn into soldiers, and they need queers and girls as the shaming contrasts against which those soldiers will be created. In other words, soldiers aren't sissies and they aren't pussies, either. These disparagements are used as behavior regulators in military settings. Military public schools are a problem, *not* simply because "don't ask, don't tell" policies restrict the access of queers to full participation in the military, but because these schools require the active, systematic, and visible disparagement and destruction of queerness and queer lives. We reject the idea that queers should organize for access to the military that depends on our revilement for its existence, rather than for the right to privacy, the right to public life, and the right to life free from militarism.

Chicago is a city awash in the randomly, tragically spilled blood of children. We live, all of us, in a violent nation that is regularly spilling the blood of other children elsewhere. These students struck out against the increasingly common practice of students marching and growing comfortable with guns.

Another group of high school students recently ventured into San Francisco's Mission District to examine the many murals that have become crucial public art in the city. Students were listening to their music players, texting friends, snapping photographs, and shooting videos. After touring the murals of Balmy Alley and the historic mural on the side of the Women's Building, they settled on a 120-foot-long work called "Our Mission–Self-Determination for All." Dividing the historical mural into different sections, the students formed groups to research the history of the conflicts, characters, and periods depicted. In the end, this project engaged students in powerful learning in history, English, art, mathematics, and cross-cultural ethnography. They went on to develop oral histories, video productions, published articles, and their own mural art work.

And, during all of this intense work, the teachers involved were subverting, defying, or ignoring the routines and sometimes the rules of schooling. They were doing the best, the most engaged and powerful, type of education. And, even if they were not articulating it consciously, they were constructing a curriculum project that drew on powerful precedents such as Paolo Freire's education projects in Brazil and the Mississippi Freedom Schools of the 1960s. More than that, they were forging an approach to education that corresponds to the current period: rejecting top-down, technocratic, authoritarian education in favor of a globally conscious, creative, and audacious approach to schooling. Why does such powerful education have to occur in defiance of our schools? How can we understand the educational project differently? And what in today's world makes such innovations not just possible but even imperative?

§

Every human being, no matter who, is part miracle, part wonder, pulsing with the breath and beat of life, inhaling, exhaling, eating and hydrating, sweating and resting, prodded by sexual urges, evolved and evolving, shaped by genetics, twisted and gnarled and hammered by the unique experiences of living this or that singular life. What sets human beings apart is our distinct way of communicating, of creating culture and constructing shared meanings with others. Human beings are suspended in intricate webs of significance, and all that we call culture can be thought of as those webs. We weave these wondrous labyrinths, both chaotic and orderly, to convey meaning and to become intelligible to one another; and we simultaneously entangle ourselves in them, constrained, and trapped. Culture always plays this two-sided role: liberator and jailer. Enacting culture allows us to make sense with others, but it also draws a line around itself, excluding those who don't share the same interpretive signifying.

Of course, making sense is always dialogic, always only partially fulfilled, never completely understood or finished. Meaning is always negotiated, never transparent—things *mean variously*. Meaning is ever busy being born, and always delaying its rendezvous with a certain destiny.

As teachers, we must struggle to understand both the importance and the elusiveness of meaning for students and all human beings—we understand, for example, that you can't get a joke by following objective laws or logical progressions, nor can you grasp the reason for a rebellion or the workings of a school from a mathematical model. We know that knowledge is not and can never be a disembodied view from nowhere, something mechanically attained, free of perspective, point of view, or situation. We see knowledge as entangled, rooted, complex, and various. And we seek, therefore, consciousness, the root of meaning, rather than an unreasoning or automatic apparatus.

Because we see knowing as transactional and focused on lived experience, and we accept knowing as always and necessarily partial, incomplete, and contingent, there is always the danger of total relativity (maybe even indifference); on the other side lurks the danger of certainty, dogmatism, and authoritarianism. Our teacherly problem is not so bad then: There is always more to know, always something in reserve. We don't get harmony or a neat and total mushing together, but neither do we get barbed wire and electric currents. We're never exactly comfortable, but we're neither numb nor sleep-walking.

What we get is a kind of arching forward, always reaching, pursuing, longing, opening, rethinking. Always contradiction, always contingency, always new vistas and open spaces. And critical reflection. And self-criticism.

That is why we try to tack back-and-forth in our teaching between poetry and newspapers, fiction and ethnography, history and literature, math and music, the most local of local detail and the larger concentric circles of context in which everyday life is lived. The purpose is to understand our life worlds, neither to caricature nor so much to criticize. It is to expand our understanding of the sensible, to build on reason and empathy, to look toward possibility.

Because we live in a perspectival world, and diversity just *is*, teachers must struggle continuously to see more, and to see more widely. A starting point is to recognize that every student comes to the classroom with a life already under way, a set of experiences and circumstances that are *sui generis*, a story in progress. And further, the teacher can assume that each student is both the one and only who will ever walk the Earth as well as the chief expert on his or her life, each the author of a singular and unique script. Recognizing this, teachers might struggle to perform a necessary and radical reversal: becoming students of their students first, in order to become better, more attuned, more effective teachers.

This points toward dialogue, everyone listening to others with the possibility of being changed, and everyone speaking up forcefully with the possibility of being heard. You must listen and speak, learn and teach. Without freedom of expression, we are doomed to accept current dogma, received ideas, prejudice, and popular stereotypes. We can try to challenge intellectual complacency, easy belief, and received wisdom. We can also become agnostics and skeptics, questioning the presuppositions and biases of others as well as of ourselves. We invite the clash of ideas. Some debates may be straightforward, others may be full of emotion and fear and pain. We can try to create the possibility of understanding the value of tolerating sharply different points of view—an impossibility unless we allow and even encourage real differences of opinion.

In reality, teaching and learning are not discrete movements; rather, they are linked gestures, back and forth, each drawing energy and focus from the other. Engaged teaching and authentic learning come to life chiefly through dialogue.

Teaching the taboo is, in this sense, teaching the segregated and suppressed, the banned and the exiled. It's opening our eyes to the lively, dynamic moment before us. It's searching actively for something more. We are in pursuit of fulfillment, reaching for the rest of our humanity.

SEVEN.

Teaching Lives

Even after all this time
The sun never says to the earth,
"You owe me."
Look what happens with
A love like that.
It lights the whole sky.

—Hafiz, 7th-century Persian poet

We recently visited Malik Dohrn, a 30-year-old tenured 6th-grade math/science teacher in an urban junior high in Northern California. At 8:00 A.M., he's a whirlwind of purposeful energy and graceful chaos: greeting students as they make their twisty ways toward their desks, and offering a special word for each one—"How's your little sister doing today, Raphael?" "Did you remember to bring me that book you borrowed yesterday, Lucy?" "Gracie, you figured out that problem you were stuck on?" "Looking smart and ready, Hector!" "Good to see you today, good to see *you*, and, hey, it's good to be seen, too!"

Malik knew each student personally, knew something special about each one—a mother in the hospital, an after-school arrangement to remember—and recognized in his greetings the gift of each one's presence here and now. Once class started, he introduced us as his dad and his uncle, and the class smiled and said hello, several noting that we were impossible to tell apart, that we must be twins.

Malik passed out simple probability problems to each table, and asked the groups of five or six to work together, and to ask for his help only if they couldn't agree among themselves. As the class buzzed along and he circulated from table to table, it became apparent that Malik also knew where each kid was in relation to the math concepts they were tackling: One had technical skills but missed the big picture, while another was entirely lost in the weeds.

Three class periods and about 50 kids later, we took Malik to lunch. It was clear to us that Malik is a great teacher, although he says of himself, "Don't call me a great teacher; I'm in here every day doing the best I can, just trying to be a better teacher." Yes, it's true, and that modesty and sense of ongoing challenge is part of his greatness in the classroom. One thing was obvious: Nothing we witnessed that morning that embodied greatness or excellence—the passion, the deep regard for the lives of the kids, the way he could challenge and nourish his students with the same gesture—will be captured on a standardized test.

We asked Malik if he thought the Secretary of Education had ever been in a real-life classroom like his. "I have a theory," he responded. "No matter what you experienced or once knew about life in classrooms, when you become an administrator, a researcher, or a policy wonk, you are force-fed a little pill that erases all traces of it from your consciousness—no memory, no know-how, no sense. You become a blank slate." We laughed and he added: "There are two classes of folks in the current school debates: people who teach, like me, and people who talk about teaching." He paused, and then finished the thought. "No offense, but you guys are both in the talk-about-it class." Ouch!

When we returned to his school, we passed through the office and Malik signed in, and then picked up a pink slip from his mailbox: He would be laid off in 90 days. We freaked, but he took it all in stride: The whole school got pink slips, and not for the first time. "Hopefully the budget will get straightened out soon, but you never know. . . ." Back to work.

Teachers are continually asked why they choose teaching, and never with as much intensity and urgency as now. The question can mean: "Why teach, when you could do something more profitable?" or "Why teach, since teaching is beneath your skill and intelligence?" Today, it increasingly means, "Why teach, when you have to put up with such relentless disrespect, the endless attacks, and the chronic uncertainty?"

Malik's case is a single story, but even a casual look into the wider world reveals a pattern that's hard to deny:

- In February 2010, the entire staff at Central Falls High School in Rhode Island was fired as part of a turn-around strategy. Central Falls is the poorest city in the state, with 41% of youngsters living in poverty and two-thirds of the high school kids qualifying for free or reduced lunch. The high school graduates a dismal 48% of its students. President Obama and Secretary of Education Arne Duncan immediately embraced the mass firing as an indication that the administration was "serious about reform." Of course, they didn't know any more about the actual situation than we did—who were the good teachers? Who were incompetent? What was being done about the various impacts of poverty on the kids? What about firing the principal or the board? No, none of that apparently mattered; none of it was worth a conversation. School failure and school problems can always be reduced to an easy answer: We must fire the bad teachers.

- On March 15, 2010, *Newsweek* magazine ran a cover story called "Why We Must Fire Bad Teachers." [49] The cover art featured a chalkboard with the repeating phrase, "We must fire bad teachers," with a headline in bold: "THE KEY TO SAVING AMERICAN EDUCATION." No one could possibly miss the message, and yet the article itself, by Evan Thomas and Pat Wingert, would hardly warrant a passing grade as a college essay: It is filled with assertions disconnected from evidence ("Some educational experts have noticed an uptick in the academic quality of new teachers . . ."); it makes sweeping and unexamined claims ("in recent years researchers have discovered something that may seem obvious, but for many years was overlooked or denied. What really makes a difference, what matters more than the class size or the textbook, the teaching method or the technology, or even the curriculum, is the quality of the teacher."); it repeats the worst clichés, myths, received wisdom, and deception ("It is difficult to dislodge the educational establishment. In New Orleans, a hurricane was required: since Katrina, New Orleans has made more educational progress than any other city, largely because the public-school system was wiped out."). Relying on neither evidence nor argument, the article utterly fails to quantify the "bad teacher" phenomenon, and paints with the broadest and most reckless brush a vision of "school failure" as belonging to teachers, and no one else.

- On November 26, 2008, *Time* magazine featured Michelle Rhee, CEO (to stay with the business metaphor of all things education today) of Washington, D.C., schools, on its cover with the headline "How to Fix America's Schools." [50] Ms. Rhee is posed in a classroom in front of a chalkboard, holding a broom, and staring straight ahead with a no-nonsense, all-business look. The pivotal paragraph in the piece praises her for making more changes in a year and a half on the job than other school leaders, "even reform-minded ones," make in five: closing 21 schools (15% of the total), firing 100 central office personnel, 270 teachers, and 36 principals. These are all policy moves that are held on faith to stand for improvement. There is not one word on kids' learning or engagement with school, not even a nod at evidence that might connect these moves with student progress, not a mention of getting greater resources into this starving system, nor parent involvement, and so on. In fact, the article characterizes any reform not focused on teachers and their unions (class size, curriculum, poverty, hunger, violence) as being "like diplomats touring a refugee camp and talking about the need for nicer curtains." But Rhee was with Teach for America for 2 years, an experience that convinced her that good teachers were the key to school improvement, according to the article; Rhee claims that kids made dramatic improvements in her class (the piece notes that there are no good data to check this lofty self-assessment), but that what broke her heart was "to watch those kids go off into the fourth grade and just lose everything."

- The *New Yorker* magazine ran an article called "The Rubber Room: The Battle over New York's Worst Teachers" on August 31, 2009.[51] It featured a site in the central bureaucracy where teachers report when they have been removed from their duties and are awaiting arbitration that will settle their status permanently. It's a thick description of a kind of purgatory for 15 teachers (there are, according to the piece, hundreds more held in large "rubber rooms" around the city), and it invites a bit of lip-smacking fascination with an oddly compelling collection of outcasts. But it is, after all, 15 teachers—that's right, in a system of 40,000. And it turns out that there's no battle at all, only a nod to due process, an exercise that is a little clumsy on all sides. But buried deep in the article is this: Before teachers got organized, they "endured meager salaries, tyrannical principals, witch hunts for Communists, and gender discrimination against a mostly female work force. . . ." Still, it's those "bad teachers" and their self-interested unions that wreak havoc on the schools.

- Davis Guggenheim's 2010 film *Waiting for Superman* is a slick marketing piece full of half-truths and distortions. The film suggests the problems in education are solely the fault of teachers and teacher unions, and it asserts that the solution to those problems is a greater focus on top-down instruction driven by test scores. It rejects the inconvenient truth that our schools are being starved of funds and other necessary resources and instead opts for an era of privatization and market-driven school change. Its focus effectively suppresses a more complex and nuanced discussion of what it might actually take to leave no child behind, such as a living wage, a full-employment economy, the de-militarization of our schools, and an education based on the democratic ideal that the fullest development of each is the condition for the full development of all. The film is positioned to become a leading voice in framing the debate on school reform, much like Guggenheim's *An Inconvenient Truth* did for the discussion of global warming, and that's heartbreaking.

Incidentally, no one argues to hold onto bad teachers, so there's something weird going on when the powerful and the noisy keep beating that straw man to death, and when nothing else is ever up for discussion. Newspapers in a dozen major cities have launched investigative reports in the last 2 years to expose "incompetent teachers" who have continued to teach; the *New York Times* has run a stream of editorials promoting an agenda of "accountability" to ferret out the bad teachers; and during the last presidential campaign, politician after politician stood up on the stump and said, "We need to get the lazy, incompetent teachers out of the classroom." Of course, whenever that phrase was uttered, all over the country people nodded dully. Who, after all, will stand up to demand that their children deserve the lazy and the incompetent? The speaker wins the point by creating the frame that will drive the audience toward the manufactured consensus.

Incidentally, if we'd got to the podium first we might have said, "Every public school kid deserves an intellectually curious, morally literate, caring and compassionate, well-rested, and well-paid teacher in the classroom." We'd have gotten the nods, too. So, in part, the problem is about who gets to set the agenda and set the frame?

Challenging the controlling discourse is always a risky business—it involves disrupting unanticipated but linked fields, and it raises related questions. If universal health care is a human right as opposed to a product, what else might be? If gay people deserve equal treatment before the law as recognizable and fully human beings, what other groups of people will expect the same? If the "war on terror" is a myth, what else in our public life is rendered unreliable? We enter an open space of rethinking and negotiation—

a space where we must rely not on rules so much as on our moral intuition, our commitment to the dignity of persons, our belief in equality, and, yes, our re-ordered and evolving common sense.

In the contested space of schools and education reform, the controlling metaphor posits education as a commodity rather than a right and a journey, and it imagines schools as little factories cranking out products, and teachers as glorified clerks or line employees, interchangeable functionaries whose job it is to pass along the wisdom and the thinking of some expert, academic, or policy-maker: Here is the literary canon; here is the truth of history; here is the skill of reading. Education as a commodity reduces teaching to the simple and efficient delivery of the package called curriculum. There is little need for adjustment, no need for dialogue. The teacher is near the base of the educational hierarchy, just above the student, who is the very bottom of the barrel.

Years ago, there was serious talk of making the curriculum "teacher proof," creating bundles of knowledge that even thoughtless, careless people could pass along. The idea behind "new math," for example, was that teachers would transmit something they neither experienced nor understood, and that a generation of brilliant mathematicians would somehow emerge, bypassing teachers altogether. This was, of course, a monumental failure, and while the rhetoric has changed—been rebranded—the substance remains the same. The current enthusiasm for some imagined artificial intelligence that will replace the need for thinking, warm-blooded, and committed teachers in classrooms is only the most recent high-tech version of the old idea of teacher-as-clerk.

The importance of this cannot be overstated: In a democracy, everyday people are sovereign; we are the ones who are charged to make the decisions that affect our lives. If we are always constrained by misinformation, lies, half-truths, and meaningless or narrowed alternatives, our imaginations wither and we find it increasingly difficult to think of alternatives to the way things are. Our lives are then controlled and manipulated. And in this context the attack on teaching and teachers is powerfully dangerous.

In 2006, Florida passed an education bill that included provisions to teach American history "as factual, not as constructed" and "as knowable, teachable, and testable." This is flatly the outlawing of critical thought. Nebraska, Arizona, Texas (and the list lengthens) have all passed laws insisting that youth be trained and even "inculcated" in the values of capitalism, "Americanism," and patriotism. What should a Japanese teacher do if the textbooks she is given ignore the 1937 Nanking massacre? What should a French teacher do if the textbooks erase the Vichy regime? These are the far-out examples, but there is much more, and it goes to the heart of what education could and should be.

If we see human beings as works-in-progress who naturally make mistakes and grow through reflection and correction, we should get rid of textbooks and anything else that claims a static and durable purchase on the Truth. We must honor language and reality by asking questions, using metaphors, and learning to use words in appropriate and innovative ways. If we see our society as necessarily an imperfect human construction, always in need of repair and renewal, our responsibility is to keep struggling to make it into one that we will all be proud to call our own. If we recognize our country as multicultural and embrace diversity as strength, we should study, appreciate, and support the never-ending human rights struggles of workers, queers, women, Blacks, other people of color, and of all Americans, which is at the heart of U.S. history, and we should demand an end to segregated schools. And as we come to our senses as the crew of Spaceship Earth, we note that all of us, and especially the young, need multiple entry points to become involved in solving neighborhood and city problems as part of their curriculum.

The challenging intellectual work of teaching pivots on our ability to see the world as it is, and simultaneously to see our students as three-dimensional creatures—human beings much like ourselves—with hopes and dreams, aspirations, skills, and capacities; with minds and hearts and spirits; with embodied experiences, histories, and stories to tell of a past and a possible future; with families, neighborhoods, cultural surrounds, and language communities all interacting, dynamic, and entangled; with the capacity to comprehend and transform the world they've been thrust into. This knotty, complicated challenge requires us to develop dispositions of patience, curiosity, respect, wonder, awe, reverence, and more than a small dose of humility. It demands sustained focus, intelligent judgment, inquiry and investigation. It calls forth an open heart and an inquiring mind since every judgment is contingent, every view partial, and each conclusion tentative.

The challenge involves, as well, an ethical stance and an implied moral contract. The good teacher offers unblinking recognition and attention, and communicates a deep regard for students' lives, a respect for both their integrity and their vulnerability. She begins with a belief that each student is unique, each the one and only who will ever trod the Earth, each worthy of a certain reverence. Regard extends, importantly, to the wider community—the wide, wide world that animates each individual life—and an insistence that students have access to the tools with which to negotiate and then to transform all that lies before them. Love for students just as they are—without any drive or advance toward a future—is false love, enervating and disabling. The teacher must try, in good faith, to do no harm, and then to convince students to reach out, to re-invent, and to seize an education fit for the fullest lives they might hope for. Another part of the work of teachers, then, is to see ourselves as in transition, in motion, works-in-progress.

Teaching against the rigid and the arid is characterized by a spirit of cooperation, inclusion, social engagement, and full participation, and classrooms become places that honor diversity while building unity. Democracy is based, after all, on the profoundly radical notion that every human being is of incalculable value, that each is unique and distinct and still part of a wildly diverse whole, and that altogether we are, each and every one, somehow essential. We recognize, then, that the fullest development of all is the condition for the full development of each, and conversely, that the fullest development of each is the condition for the full development of all. This core principle has fundamental implications for educational politics and policy, and powerful implications for curriculum and teaching as well, for what is taught and how.

Excellent teaching is sustained through a culture of respect and mutual recognition that encourages students to develop the capacity to name the world for themselves, to identify the obstacles to their (and other people's) full humanity, and the courage to act upon whatever the known demands. This kind of education is necessarily earth-shaking—it is seen as a step toward the taboo—always about opening doors and opening minds as students forge their own pathways into a wider, shared world.

We learn to live in dialogue, speaking with the possibility of being heard, and listening with the possibility of being changed. We learn to ask many kinds of essential questions again and again, and then find ways to live within and beyond the answers we receive: What's your story? Who are you in the world? How did you (and I) get this far? What do we know now? What do we have the right to imagine and expect? Where are we going? Who decides? Who's left out? What are the alternatives? Why? In many ways, these kinds of questions are themselves the answers, for they lead us into a powerful sense that we can and will make a difference.

We gesture toward the personal, the particular, the integrated, the supportive, even as we remain mindful of the social and the shared, the global and the political. We point toward students at the center of the educational enterprise, every student known well by some caring adult, and every student with the real possibility of belonging to a community of learners. There is, then, a sense of visibility, of significance, of the hope to negotiate here the tricky terrain of identity. The message to children and youth is clear: In this classroom and at this moment, you are a valuable and valued person; without you, this entire enterprise would flounder and fail.

Education, like love, is generative: The more you have, the better off you become; the more you give away, the more you have. Open hearts, open doors, open minds: Giving knowledge and learning and education away diminishes nothing.

We turn to the themes of liberation pedagogy linked to broad social movements. Students become the subjects and the actors in constructing their own educations, not simply the objects of a regime of discipline and punish. Education becomes uncoupled from the inadequate and illegitimate "meritocracy model," and the public good becomes understood more fundamentally. Instead of schooling-as-credentialing, sorting, gate-keeping, and controlling, education allows *all* students to become smarter, more capable of negotiating our shared and complex world, more able to work effectively in community and across communities to innovate and initiate with courage and creativity. We all begin to re-examine core personal and ethical values in order to make more thoughtful, caring, and productive life choices. This requires courage—from teachers, families, communities, and students—to build alternative and insurgent schools focused on what we know we need rather than what we are told we must endure.

Starting from their own interests and concerns, drawing occasionally on pre-industrial traditions such as rites of passage, students can co-create curriculum in both classrooms and community, as they broaden their insights into projects that serve the people. Classroom walls will be knocked down and students will merge into cities and countryside to do community building, and social transformation, exploration, organizing, rethinking and rebuilding and re-culturing, working toward a new praxis.

All of this and more is already happening as part of the shifting of the discourse and the shifting of power in the world. Bob Moses argues that the struggle for a people's education must become the watchword of organizing, a fundamental demand just as "one person/one vote" was 40 years ago.[52] Students already make video, radio, newspapers, music, and journals. They publish their findings and their questions, and their creative insights are shared everywhere. As with break dancing, hip-hop, graffiti, slamming, and crunching, young people always find their own unique ways to invent their identities and express their yearnings and their resistance. And, of course, massive corporate machines are put into overdrive in attempts to co-opt and control the thinking of young minds; they, too, become part of the contested space.

Youth today cross borders, reappropriate media, make their own meanings, and free up formerly controlled spaces. If educators are to be rescued from utter irrelevance, we must meet young people where their literacy, their meaning-making, their imaginations are unleashed. Teachers are invited to relinquish their roles as arbiters of value and to transform themselves into coaches and allies of students, enabling projects to reach ever farther into the community. Math, science, language, sports, literature, music, art, and history can all be explored in cross-curricular projects that extend between classes and between alternate learning sites.

While the educational system was trudging along, putting kids to sleep, complaining about the students, many have initiated projects outside of the schools that engaged young people and that elicited the creativity and leadership of those who had been written off as educationally at risk. Youth Radio and Youth Speaks, for example, were not driven by a secret plan to raise test scores or participate in anything to do with a traditional school trajectory. They grew up to fill a niche, a hole in youth lives that was obvious to anyone who looked. They pursued interests that were burning in the young themselves.

These young people wanted their voices out there. While some could put graffiti on buildings and trains, if they had a chance, they would most love to represent their realties out in the even wider world. Instead of treating kids as amateurs, errors, and problems, there are a range of projects that recognize youth as they ignite their own perspectives, their own fresh ideas.

Youth Radio gave them access to radio—for their own type of news and commentary, for beats and music. Youth Radio provided equipment, access to professional media people, and a safe space to learn. Through a process of peer teaching, a progression through ever higher levels of skill and responsibility, and an enthusiasm for youth-generated content, Youth Radio unleashed a process of teen engagement that is training thousands and thousands of young people, pioneering alternate access to audiences, and along the way winning dozens of journalism awards. Elisabeth Soep and Vivian Chávez have explored the process of converged literacies and collegial pedagogy that are being invented in these spaces.[53]

Youth Speaks channeled the exploding culture of hip-hop into massive poetry sessions—moving them from polite tea parties to auditorium-sized rallies. Instead of telling them what to do, Youth Speaks adopted the slogan "Because the next generation can speak for themselves." Instead of asking kids to fill in the bubbles, it asked students to explore who they were, what they cared about, how they understood the world, and where they wanted to go next. Youth Speaks honored the culture and helped young people gain tools and skills, allowed them to apprentice next to more experienced poets, and showed them how to become adept at revision and redrafting.

Both of these projects reach a range of people of all races, ethnicities, and incomes. But they have particularly served marginalized communities and have shown how African American and Chicano-Latino students can be successful leaders by putting in charge those who have been scorned by officials. They have been supportive and safe spaces for women and LGBTQ youth to excel and take leadership. And they have been a site of diversity, demonstrating how our society could be if youth had the power and the agency to shape it.

When we look at initiatives such as Youth Radio and Youth Speaks, each of which now has projects going around the country, we realize that we must look outside of the schoolhouse walls for models of engaged, demo-cratic education. Why not wonder who else has something to tell us? We could start with Studs Terkel, who took the radical discourse of Depression-era organizers to a new kind of journalism—honoring the voice, the insight, and the genius of the man (and woman) on the street, of the common man (and woman). Studs, who died in 2008, famously followed Brecht's dictum to wonder about the story not of the pharaohs and their great accomplish-ment, but of the workers who toiled their whole lives at the base. Who built the pyramids? Who suffered in the wars? Who has dreams and hopes that might tell us something? Ever the curious intellectual, Studs did not neglect the classic philosophers and artists. He simply found their truths and more in the lives and stories of everyone. He elicited, through his curiosity and his insistence on listening, listening honestly and open-heartedly, to people, the subversive truths of those who are ignored in the discourse of power.

Anna Deavere Smith, a contemporary actress and teacher, continues and extends Studs Terkel's work. She constructs dramatic performances—usually one-woman shows—based on extensive interviews with participants and witnesses to history. Her plays have her capturing the voice, manner-isms, and nuances of each person she has encountered. She wades into the most divisive and complicated conflicts in our society, civil strife, health care, racism, and community. Again, she suggests to us some important things about teaching. There is always wisdom in every room; the answer is not in one dogma or one story—it is in the kaleidoscope of perspectives, interests, needs, and longings. Like Studs Terkel, Anna Deavere Smith can go from the mundane tale of a routine day in life to an exploration of the human heart, our deepest ethical concerns, and the challenges we face to lead lives of purpose and meaning.

Where else might we look for that subversive, that critical perspective in our culture? Comedy has always served as the voice of the marginalized, the challenge to received wisdom. Like a little court jester on our shoulders, it challenges us to question the master narrative. Whether it was the Yiddish vaudeville comedians of the 1920s or Moms Mabley in the 1950s, comedians have ridiculed the emperor and his new clothes. Who carries on the tradition? Who has something to teach teachers? Richard Pryor, of course, and also Margaret Cho. Jon Stewart, Dave Chapelle, and Stephen Colbert have become the voice of truth in a dreary period of official lies. We stand in front of classes and deliver the official line, and the kids go home and watch *South Park* or Adult Swim, deconstructing and ridiculing everything. Is it anarchistic? Indeed it is. So were the Marx Brothers.

Our job is not to teach against these perspectives. It is especially not to teach against them and go home at night and secretly chuckle at the comic take-down of our day jobs. It is to let everyone in on the joke, let a hundred guffaws bloom, and perhaps come out with a curriculum that is a little less self-righteous and a little more fun—taboo, and true.

EIGHT.

Release the Wisdom in the Room: Language and Power

Precisely because I do not have/ the beautiful words I need/ I call upon my acts/ to speak to you.

—Daisy Zamora, *Life for Each*

For many teachers, stuck in schools that value narrow, quantifiable out-comes in the form of test scores, the good stuff—the real student learning and human development—happens in the margins, off the script, in clubs or after school and without official acknowledgment. When we meet up with students much later and savor the best of our years together, we don't wax nostalgic over the standardized test results that were achieved. We recall the debate in the hall, the fellow student who was in deep crisis, the break-through achieved during a retreat.

But the best stuff doesn't have to be relegated to back-channel, unof-ficial interactions in schools. If we have the courage and determination to create together, we can inspire generative centers where curiosity is unleashed and community enacted. The key is to unlock the genius, the enthusiasm and creativity in the room so that everyone there, too, is clam-oring for the mic.

Poetry slams started sweeping schools at the end of the 1990s, taking root on campuses where students and teachers had seen the documentary *Slamnation* or learned of the open-mic nights at the Green Mill in Chicago or the Nuyorican Poets Café in New York. Soon organizations such as

Youth Speaks were making connections and planting new seeds, developing regional and national competitions among youth poets.

Why competition? That seems something odd to inject into poetry. There is no good answer. But it is clear the involvement of the audience and judges in reviewing publicly declaimed poems has turned youth poetry from a quiet, soft event of imitative and pretentious verse to an exciting evening of collective engagement and excitement, much like an athletic event. English teachers sit in awe as they watch their students working long hours to get a poem to bring to the slam, building powerful images and insights into poems that have immediate impact. This comes from students who have often resisted classroom assignments, and now suddenly authentic and vibrant literacy is bursting out all over.

Why? What happened? We certainly can't take credit for this explosion of literacy activity. Suddenly, poetry was cool. Where young men used to mark themselves as most available through sports, now you could get laid by being a great slam poet. It was actually a natural outgrowth of rapping in hip-hop music, a tradition that goes back to the griot and the epic poets, up through blues singers and the Last Poets. The groundwork for the poetry slam phenomenon was laid by the wild popularity of hip-hop. Indeed, it was not at all unusual to see teenagers who had memorized thousands of lines of hip-hop, many thousands of lines, while they continued to fail in English class. Something outside of the curriculum, outside of the walls, swept students into performance, into extensive reading and writing.

Slam poetry surprised us in other ways. In schools that were fiercely divided by race or cliques, the slam was the most integrated and united space around. The African American boy with street corner tales of daring and horror, the Latina with angry insight, the diminutive White freshman who recites his poem, "Recipe for a Homosexual"—they all listen closely and applaud one another. The competition aspect, the scoring and second round and ultimate winners—this gives the evening a sense of drama, a story arc of a whole narrative in which each poem played a role. But ultimately, the poetry holds it own and the poetry is remembered.

The poetry slam phenomenon is one of those "outsider" literacy activities that the schools regard with suspicion or even hostility. Progressive teachers see them as a way to hook kids, to draw them back to the curriculum in the traditional classroom. Perhaps both are wrong—the first for obvious reasons, but the second because they can only see this practice as something of a leverage to bring kids back to the classroom that has failed them and often banished them.

There's something at once sincere and clueless about the way foundations and outreach groups approach the youth out-of-school expressions of literacy and fund them to pull kids back to school. Adults are searching for the next creative site of authenticity, always with the purpose of harnessing it for traditional school. This comes from a worthy impulse, of course, but we ought to seriously wonder why youth keep running outside of the walls to do deep, committed work. The problem, again, is not with the youth but with the stultifying institutions that have failed to offer them engagement or authenticity.

We address this contradiction, this mismatch of purposes, directly with our students. This is not simply a teacher's dilemma—it is a subject to share with the class, to explore honestly. If we have only the best interests of the students in mind, we want them to understand the codes of power, to get through the gatekeepers, to get onto the next steps in their lives. But, in order to hold on to this position, we often patronize student thinking and dismiss the way they represent the world. Some would like to get that professional job 10 years down the line. But many have done the math and know damn well that all 3,000 students in this inner-city school are not going to college, the 150,000 high school students in this city are not going to college. Get real. There are not enough spaces. So are the teachers actually cheering for their own students, in hopes that they beat out the kids in the next inner-city school? What about those who will be left behind?

Carol Lee engages these issues in her discussion of "Cultural Modeling," the importance of accessing generative cultural data sets—insights, texts, practices—from student life in order to develop habits and procedures for addressing complex problems.[54] The regime of rote learning to which oppressed students are relegated leaves them poorly prepared for anything—whether imagining a different world or simply developing creative approaches to answering questions on a test. Cultural Modeling honors the belief systems, cultural practices, and ways of using the language of students—recognizing that the "vernacular practices" of African American, Chicano-Latino, and other students who have been scorned by the educational establishment are, in fact, intellectually rich. This is not to valorize slang or to stand back and imagine that great intellectual work will happen with no intervention or connection whatsoever. Instead, it is a commitment to access the brilliance in the room toward a common, and authentic, project.

Marv Hoffman has faced this issue in his reevaluation of the famous "Letters to a Teacher" essay by the Schoolboys of Barbiana in Italy in the 1960s.[55] The Barbiana students were all from poor and peasant families; they had been scorned, marginalized, and pushed out of school. The teacher in their new school, a radical priest named Father Milani, created a writing project for them that consisted of letters addressed to their former teachers. By sharing these letters, the boys created a single document, a manifesto, really, that enumerated the failings of Italian schooling. And, in the course of this authentic writing project, they found their voices and became stronger students.

But part of the radicalism of the project was that the students rejected the single-minded pressure to go into professions, to go to college. Yes, some did in the end. But they also looked at how to live, how to be effective members of the working class and to use their skills to fight for that class. Too often, the goal of progressive teachers is to get kids "out of the ghetto," out of the working class—to make them, in other words, more like us. Certainly, we want choices for everyone, but we question why everything we touch we turn into another impulse away from the working class, away from the diverse lives of real families, away from parents and away from home. There are alternatives.

Pedro Noguera, one of the great advocates of successful educational projects in urban schools, argues that liberal teachers who seek to rescue youth from the ghetto are essentially on a charity, redemptive project. What is really needed is solidarity, an approach that helps youth imagine ways to transform their communities. And, no doubt, given the many ways in which the cards are stacked against that transformation (patterns of housing, jobs, and prisons, for example), it takes quite a creative leap to begin to see how to get started. This is precisely why urban education must go beyond the drill and discipline regimen, must be centered on creativity, imagination, and the arts. For in the arts, after all, we are not tied to the plodding and demoralizing of the world as it is. We reconstruct, reappropriate, repurpose our world and make a mix that works for us.

Something else the arts teach: It's not about getting the correct answer. It's about getting it wrong, again and again, and recognizing each misstep and wrong choice as the path to the next beautiful creation. An education that puts arts in the center encourages resilience, agency, passion, and a sense of humor. This will turn out to be the heart of "21st-century skills," not the narrow technical knowledge of computer programs as defined by district mission statements.

In a democratic classroom, as in a poetry slam or a hip-hop radio show, everyone is clamoring for the mic. Notice the teachers as they listen to students, invite student stories, analyze those stories for common themes and human meaning, and make a plan to act. The discourse communities that the students come from bring much of the wisdom, the talent, and the analytical power to reshape the world. Teachers might find ways to move their classrooms from being sites of invalidation to centers of community organizing.

Teaching is often construed as passing down, the transmission of some knowledge, some information, some procedures that the teacher knows and the students lack. All the grammar of education literature, from the action verbs of handing over, delivering, showing, and telling, to the objects of the sentences, invariably the students, forces us to think this way. Anything else is just fuzzy-headed chaos, touchy-feely idealism.

This debate has gone all the way back in American education. The struggle between the principle of authoritative knowledge handed down by those in power and the democratic practice of developing knowledge through social interaction was acted out soon after the American Revolution. When Daniel Webster dedicated the memorial to the martyrs of Bunker Hill, he invoked the importance of the founding fathers as the authority to which all patriotic citizens had to defer. Ralph Waldo Emerson (and later Frederick Douglass), however, chastised Webster. Eduardo Cadava explains,

> Webster's identification of this power with the past as well as with himself works to seduce the audience into obedience. Emerson, by contrast, identifies this power with nature and suggests that it is available to the "race of children" in the same way it was available to their fathers. The adherence to revolutionary principles, for him, should promote the virtue of self-reliance rather than the weakness of dependence. [56]

Webster, we recall, went on to support the Fugitive Slave Act while Emerson and Douglass deeply opposed it.

And Henry David Thoreau[57] went further than Emerson in extolling natural and immanent sensing in order to understand the world—a philosophy opposed to received wisdom and traditional authority. Thoreau condemned the blindness and conformity of those in power. In all his writing, Thoreau calls on the readers to take power over their lives, to achieve their own freedom. In his view of education, to teach is not to impose a code or way of life; rather, it is to enable students to learn. It is ironic that Thoreau is today placed in authoritative examination questions when he argued that he preferred an education through "perpetual suggestions and provocations." Thoreau argued in his journal that "we reason from our hands and our head."

Herman Melville, too, anticipates Mark Twain in his utter disdain for the hypocrisies of traditional authorities, organized religion, and the catechism of formulaic learning. Both Thoreau and Melville are fascinated with the developments in natural science, close observation, classification, and the induction of an ecstatic philosophy of natural law—based on feelings, insight, and epiphanies.

In the 19th century, we find the "other" stepping up with his (and her) own voice, particularly in the struggle of African Americans, first against slavery, and then for the rights of citizenship. Frederick Douglass was the leading African American political figure of the 19th century. W.E.B. DuBois described the educational project for liberation in "The Public Schools" chapter of *Black Reconstruction in America*. He describes the extensive work of the Freedmen's Bureau in the South after the war when, protected by Union military forces, some of them Black, a great explosion of democracy took place. The Reconstruction acts included the founding of the first public schools (for White and Black children). Many White Northern women, who had been trained in such institutions as the Troy Female Seminary, braved the dangers of the South to staff these first schools.

Educational leaders included Booker T. Washington, the founder of Tuskegee Institute in Alabama. His approach was for training newly freed slaves to find jobs within the expanding industrial economy. DuBois, in a series of polemics and in his seminal *Souls of Black Folk*, engaged the Washington approach, accusing it of making Black workers passive tools to the wealthy rather than helping them realize their full humanity, citizenship, and equality. Like the Chicago reformer Jane Addams, DuBois was critical of the drive in schools to create industrial discipline and impersonality.

All of these struggles pitted the notion of a broad, democratic education arising from the culture of the people against the authoritarian notion of what John Dewey called abstract object lessons, passive listening, which construes knowledge as an immobile solid.

Today's authoritarians are the product of the 30-year Reagan-Bush era, which peddled "free" markets while imposing a regime of repression, militarization abroad, and imprisonment at home. Since their dreams of a unipolar world, an unchallenged American empire, have been frustrated, we have a chance today to recoup some sense of balance, a culture of possibility and solidarity.

An important way to bring this discussion, this dilemma, into the classroom is to invite students to examine discourse—cultural language practices. Given the invitation, students are brilliant at exploring the different discourses that are in the room and the official discourse of schooling. The concept of discourse analysis, vernacular, the evolution of ratified and low-status discourses, and code switching come easily to students who live this reality every day.

Richard Rodriguez, in his autobiography, examines the long and lonely path to school success for him, a young child of immigrants in Los Angeles.[58] He was not the troubled or the resistant student. He describes himself as the super-achiever, the "scholarship boy," the exception to his peers. And yet, he realizes many years later, each success that welcomed him into the cool rationality of school took him farther away from the warm and garrulous world of his parents. He regrets now his cruelties, correcting his parents' English, impatient with the conversations at home. Richard Rodriguez gained a great deal by being a successful student, but he also lost something—his working-class home and family.

He says more than this, though. Rodriguez recognizes that, although he was a compliant and hard-working student, he was also a very bad student. Intimidated and imitative, he failed to offer opinions of his own. He plowed through books with determination but never brought his own point of view or stance to the text. So the problem of discourse and power continued to dominate this young student, even as he succeeded and rejected his parents. Ultimately, he was able to come full circle and use his acquired skills to name this dilemma. But what of our students, the ones who will and the ones who won't go on to college? In response to Rodriguez, generations of students have written passionate and insightful papers about their own journeys through schooling—journeys fraught with struggle and complexity. Students are struggling to maintain, and to construct, their own identities within an institution that validates White middle-class student discourse as a matter of routine and puts all others into deep conflict.

This outsider status, constructed marginal status that is inscribed in language practices, recalls the insight of Jacques Derrida that, as a Pied Noir French colonial raised in Algeria, and a Jew, he was a man who spoke only French, but French was not his language. Official, state-endorsed French, the language of power, its inflections and implications, is not his, is like a second language to him. "I have only one language yet it is not mine. . . . [T]he only language I speak is *not mine*; I did not say it was foreign to me."[59]

Educators—those responsible to help students enjoy literature, arts, and poetry—face a contradiction since their role requires them to act as police for the state in this interdiction of the language of the other, of the outsider. Pierre Bourdieu explains that

> The official language is bound up with the state, both in its genesis and in its social uses . . . the linguistic law has a body of jurists—the grammarians—and its agents of regulation and imposition—the teachers—who are empowered

universally to subject the linguistic performance of speaking subjects to examination and to the legal sanction of academic qualification.[60]

This problem of official language and the outsider language is reminiscent of W.E.B. DuBois's discussion of "double consciousness" of African American people in the United States. Colonization through language is precisely the experience of the Vietnamese and Senegalese (French), the Brazilians (Portuguese), and the South Asians (English). Often, in attempting to assimilate and access the language of power, the colonial becomes "more French than the French," an observation also extended to English in India. But it is also true within the United States, where the language of power, of legitimacy, is precisely the creation of a sense of other, of outsider status, in African American, Chicano-Latino, and immigrant students.

According to Derrida, the master language is distant, uninhabitable, and deserted: "The language called maternal is never purely natural, nor proper, nor habitable."[61] What would happen if the master language, the official voice, is triumphant and the marginalized, the ones who bend and twist and bring alive the language, are exterminated? This is precisely the fate of Germany after the Holocaust. Having eliminated the Jews, the Germans were left with a language community that was all standard, that took some decades to bring back to life.

Issues of power and access of the language of power are explored in extensive discussion and theorizing about Ebonics, or African American Vernacular English. Besides the extensive work done by Perry and Delpit (1998), we find Black youth discourse examined in Ibrahim's "Wassup Homeboy? Joining the African Diaspora: Black English as a Symbolic Site of Identification and Language Learning" (Makoni, 2003). In addition, Toni Morrison, in *Playing in the Dark* (1992), defines the outsider role of African American arts and writing. Like the Magic Realists of the last century, like African and African American cultural critics today, the new communities, the new alignments of youth, are redefining the ways of knowing the world and the ways of expressing their world. They access deep roots in African and Indigenous cultures but not as primordialist retreats. Rather, these are ways of going forward, of mixing imagination, what Appadurai calls nostalgia for the present, and a determination for independence and community. Post-colonial theorists such as Homi Bhabha, C.L.R. James, and S. Kaviraj examine ways that oppressed peoples contest the hegemony of the dominant discourse.

From here, it is easy to jump to further explorations. Students are fascinated to write down overheard conversations, to examine oral language and dialogue in films and novels, to write papers in their own "home" vernacular. And classes can examine the broader issues of equity and education, reading articles by Lisa Delpit, Victoria Purcell Gates, Glynda Hull, and Jabari Mahiri. High school students develop their own critique of language and power practices in school and, like the schoolboys of Barbiana, they take ownership of the curriculum.

And they are not alone. The great fiction being written today does not bow down to the master discourse, does not pledge obedience to school-bound, straitjacketed English. Junot Diaz's Pulitzer Prize–winning *The Brief, Wondrous Life of Oscar Wao* is a wild ride into the real discourse, the multiple-voiced reality, of Dominican immigrant youth in New Jersey. It leaps between Ebonics, Spanglish, Dominican slang, Standard English, science-fiction lingo, classical references, and comic books. It revels in the real, the complex, the warm embrace of language as it is lived in our global communities. In a sense, its very boldness of self-expression seeks to shatter the cold grammar of control. Maximiliano, a Latino high school student, who had never finished an independent reading book before, looked up from the page after an hour of reading and declared, "I never knew these things could be put down in a book." For him, the expectation was that books would always be remote, forbidding, bristling with "No Trespassing" signs.

And many more besides Junot Diaz are up to this, the rescuing and honoring of complex vernaculars. Check out Amitav Ghosh's *Sea of Poppies*, set on a ship at harbor in Calcutta in the 1830s. It is written, however, with a deeply post-modern sensibility, celebrating the many points of view, cultures, and languages that made up Calcutta even 200 years ago. And the list goes on and on. Hip-hop revels in its take-down of the master discourse, and it has exploded in to all walks of life.

One group of students at the Communication Arts and Sciences small school at Berkeley High developed a slang dictionary as a classroom project. Each student brought in five cards with a word on each, complete with pronunciation guide, etymology (as well as could be divined), part of speech, and sample sentence. After the words were arranged in alphabetical order and typed up, they were posted on the wall—provoking extensive debate and correction until each word was acceptable to the class. This was not a project of rejecting what has been anointed as "standard" English but rather of understanding deeply the interaction of different language practices.

Through an exploration of their own discourse, students had a chance to examine their own values and culture with a new eye. They discovered that there were more slang words for "friend" than any other—as teens are deeply concerned about relationships and friendship. Drugs and sex figured large, too, but not always with confidence and familiarity, but rather as an area of daring and anxiety. Moreover, in areas of slang, the students were clearly the experts and the teacher the outsider, the amateur. Such a reversal of social capital meant that the students could show what they knew and, indeed, the teacher could model how to be a good-humored and curious learner.

After a study of language and discourse practices, student discussion as well as reading and writing was completely different. Instead of being a forbidding code fraught with pain and anger, language became something that the students analyzed and owned. Students enjoyed showing what they knew well—wisdom that had never previously been validated in the class-room—while unleashing their curiosity about other language practices without a threat to their own identity or dignity.

Students who have learned that there are language codes, that some codes (those associated with the White middle class) have more privilege, don't simply have to submit to the discourse of power. They have been let in on the joke and they learn to play, freely and creatively, across the terrain. Students learn to bring a critical eye to everything.

Here's an example. Take a look at the Depression-era photographs of Dorothea Lange—beautiful photographs, evoking insight and understanding of the terrible suffering caused by the forced migration of Oklahoma farmers to California. But then take a look, as a group of urban students did, at the photographs of Sebastião Salgado, the Brazilian who has documented forced migration of peoples all over the world. Where do the eyes go? What are they saying with their expressions? Next to the Salgado pictures, Lange's begin to look quite different. Her subjects are beaten down, discouraged, without agency or even identity.

Indeed, students do research and find that some of the "Okies" in the photographs have resented the way they were depicted, like passive victims. No, they argue, we were strong, determined, and good-humored through an arduous but adventurous journey. Lange's tragic representations were just that—the expression of a middle-class radical, a critic of the system, of the pain the people are suffering. But her photographs do not suggest that the Okies would struggle, that they would be able to win victories. Instead, they are designed to evoke pity and perhaps an outpouring of support from middle-class progressives who viewed her photographs.

Salgado's immigrants, on the other hand, although even poorer and more desperate than Lange's, look defiantly into the camera, daring us to get to know them. They look like people who are not only capable of taking on their own struggles, but ones you would feel honored to sit down and have a conversation with, to learn from them. In Lange's photographs, the photographer is telling the story and the subjects are silent; in Salgado's, the migrant-subjects are telling their own story.

Again, having students read the codes, letting them in on the joke, unleashes endless insights. The next step? It's obvious: Students must go out and do portrait photographs of their own families, their own communities. What story will their camera tell?

NINE.

Voyage to the Unknown

Optimism and hope are different. Optimism tends to be based on the notion that there's enough evidence to allow us to think things are going to be better . . . Whereas hope looks at the evidence and says it doesn't look good at all, but we're going to go beyond the evidence to create new possibilities based on visions that become contagious to allow us to engage in heroic actions always against the odds, no guarantees whatsoever.

—Cornel West

Educators face a contradiction at the heart of their efforts: The humanistic ideal, the democratic injunction, tells us that every person is an entire universe, that each can develop as a full and autonomous person engaged with others in a common polity and an equality of power; the capitalist imperative, in sharp contradiction, insists that humans are the instrument of profit-making and that profit is at the center of economic and political progress—developing a culture of competition, elitism, and hierarchy. An education for democracy fails as an adjunct to this unbridled competition—either the schools or the system must yield.

Teaching aims both to guide and to set free, to initiate *into* as well as to liberate *from*. Teaching is part prescription, part permission. Great teachers walk this fault line consciously, with courage and confidence, working to move their students into thinking for themselves, awakening in them new awarenesses, igniting their imaginations, and encouraging them to live a while in possibility, spurring them to go farther and farther. And with all this teachers simultaneously provide students with access to the tools of the culture, the structures of the disciplines, the various languages and literacies that will allow them to participate fully and freely. This is only possible when teachers present themselves as questioning, fallible, searching human beings themselves—identical in this regard to those they teach.

It is always a struggle for conscientious teachers to be true to students while keeping an eye on the world that those students will inherit. There are some common themes that can prove helpful for further thinking and rethinking, for action, and for rethinking once more:

- Teaching the taboo involves seeing students as whole human beings with hearts and minds, bodies and spirits that must somehow be taken into account. We must find our way beyond the half-language of labels.

- We must be doubly serious in our efforts to teach our students the various literacies that will allow them to become competent and powerful in their worlds.

- We must provide opportunities for students to do and to make, and to become valuable and valued in their various communities.

- We must learn *from* rather than *about* the world—from work, not about work; from democracy, not about democracy; from nature, not about nature; from history, geography, literature, math, and so on.

- We must bring the community into the school and the school into the community. Classrooms are contested spaces, and the sooner we face that fact, the more effective we might become.

An education for democracy begins with the belief that each person has the right and responsibility to participate publicly, that each can and should make a difference. The principles of associative living—community, equality, liberty—must be brought to the fore. Why should this be taboo? But it is.

We must, with our students, learn to ask the essential questions again and again, and then find ways to live within and beyond the answers we receive. Who are you in the world? How did you (and me) get here? What can we know? What do we have the right to imagine and expect? Where are we going? Who makes the decisions? Who's left out? Who decides? Who benefits? Who suffers? What are the alternatives? In many ways, these kinds of questions are themselves the answers.

Education is never neutral—even, or perhaps especially, when it insistently strikes that pose. In a dynamic, propulsive, forward-charging, expanding, and perspectival world, neutrality and objectivity are always up for grabs, and education—along with everything else—is always in the mix.

The pretense of objectivity and neutrality in education is in practice in support of the status quo, the existing state of affairs, the impossible idea that what is right now will always be. This day, this moment, this particular social order is a point of arrival–the end. Of course, a moment's reflection reveals that it can't possibly be true. Moreover, in a social system of unequal power, of hierarchy, command and control, neutrality favors domination– objectivity limits the fact of choice. Frantz Fanon famously said that for the native, objectivity is always an assault, something engaged against him, a force favoring his enforced disadvantage, and the most revolutionary act is simply questioning.

We want to think of classrooms as places of possibility, sites of hope and resistance, venues where we might live part of our dreams and glimpse, if we choose, fragments of what could be but is not yet. We want to think of classrooms as participatory places, kind and visionary, grounded in the lives of students, powered by their own curiosities and imaginations and powerful sense-making capacities–critical, wondering, trembling, and real. We want to investigate classrooms where queer questions are common, where seeking deeper understanding is the order of the day. Mostly, we're interested in classrooms where teachers and students feel themselves alive and active on an historic stage.

In Arkansas–where Governor Huckabee is the poster boy of dramatic weight loss, and a leader in the national campaign against obesity–school report cards now must include each child's BMI, or body mass index. Obesity, as you probably already know, is a massive public health problem and its dimensions have been growing for decades. Obesity is now the number-one killer disease in the United States, and today's children will be the first generation in history to fail to outlive their parent generation, chiefly because of fat. The aim of the BMI notation on the report cards is apparently to make students and parents more aware of the scale of the thing, and to encourage participation to fight it. Who could possibly object to the Arkansas initiative? Well, we could and we do.

We don't object to awareness, or to participation, but this initiative doesn't quite accomplish either. It's a broad and crude measure–like a B or a C–and it locates the heart of this decidedly *social* problem squarely within the individual rather than the public. The implied solution is private and personal rather than collective and shared. And, of course, it is personal in making a public ranking of the student. Lawmakers and police chiefs and corporate heads never have their BMI, or their test scores, or their discipline records, publicly published. Why not?

There is a possible classroom response, a curriculum reaction that begins, as always, with questioning the assumptions, the common sense, and the logic of school and public policy. Let's make the BMI notation an object of study, a case for interrogation, an issue to examine, question, and, perhaps, challenge.

In the interest of historicizing everything, we might ask two kinds of questions:

- What is the history of obesity as a health problem in the United States and elsewhere? Is it considered an "eating disorder," and if so, how is it like/unlike other "eating disorders"? What part of the problem is genetic predisposition, what part habit or education, what part access?
- What is the history of engaging schools to solve broader social problems? Why is it done and how successful has it been? What's been the result of mandating alcohol and drug awareness programs, for example, or suicide prevention and abstinence programs?

In the spirit of politicizing everything, we can go further:

- Who decided to mandate the inclusion of the BMI? Was there broad participation and dialogue by parents, students, teachers, or the broader community before the mandate was operationalized?
- Which industries suffer because of obesity, and which ones benefit? What's the relationship of fat and sugar to the problem? What public and economic policies impact the sugar industry, for example?
- Is obesity correlated in any way to income, class, race, or gender? How?
- Are exercise facilities available equally across communities regardless of income or property values? Are parks equitably distributed?
- Is the fat content of foods such as hamburger identical whether sold in a wealthy or a poor community?
- Are fruits and vegetables accessible equitably, regardless of community income?

- How has the "thin" ideal impacted women in our society?

In the spirit of active inquiry close to home, again there are more questions:

- How much time is allotted to physical education?
- Are all students equally encouraged or even required to participate in sports and games?

- What is a typical school lunch?
- What's a calorie? What's an empty calorie?
- How many calories does a typical student in this school consume and burn in a day?
- Does the school sell soda, candy, or fatty foods from vending machines? Fast food or junk food? Fruits and vegetables? Why?
- Do clubs or teams sell candy or cookies to raise funds?
- How close to the school is a restaurant, shop, store, or stand where fast food or junk food is available?
- What is the school's relationship to McDonald's, Coke, Pepsi, Dunkin' Donuts, or their parent corporations?

When a teacher took the bold step of challenging her students in one classroom one year to "pose your own problems and ask your own questions of the world you see," that single gesture opened a world of propulsive learning, new knowledge, and even a bit of unexpected wisdom. Some limited classroom time opened up for the work, but, more important perhaps, the culture and the feel of the place transformed dramatically: Kids dug into work with a spirit of curiosity and purposeful energy, questions tumbled onto each other, excitement and investment in learning went viral. Who knows where that will take them, and us? It's only a start.

Shelley: What Do You Buy Into?

- Select several familiar advertisements—clip them from magazines or write out verbatim what they say on TV or radio or billboards—and ask: What is the message? Is there more than one message? If so, what are they? Do they contradict themselves?
- Does it influence me? If so, how? Is any of it true?
- Am I part of some targeted audience? How is a targeted audience chosen? How would I know that?
- What is this advertisement telling me about my family, my place in the world, my goals and my ability to achieve them, my cultural heritage, my identity and sense of self, my community, my morality and my values, my gender role, my politics, my money, my sex, my relationships?
- Should I do anything to challenge any of this? How?
- Who makes advertising decisions? How much money was spent in this advertising campaign? What is the end goal of the ad? How far are the advertisers willing to go to achieve their goals?
- Does this affect me at all? If so, how and why? Does this affect my community in any positive or negative way? How?

- Where's the company's headquarters and manufacturing facility? Who are the employees? What are their wages? Are the wages fair? What are the working conditions like? Are they just? Is there a union? Does the company's location have an impact on wages or working conditions?
- Does any of this affect me or my community? What can or should I do about it?
- How does this company impact the environment?
- What can I do?
- How are the messages in these advertisements delivered visually and textually? Are they effective? Do any images oppress, discriminate, or slight anyone? Are any other artists or activists responding to images or messages in advertisements? Who? Who's listening? Do I have any responsibility for these messages?

Todd: What's Eating You?

- What questions do you have about food?
- Where does our school food come from? Where is it produced? What are the working conditions of the various people who produced this food? Who are the school's vendors and who decides who they will be? How much does it cost? Which food is eaten and how much is wasted? What other food is available? Do we have vending machines? What kinds of foods do kids bring from home?
- What food do other kids in other schools get? Is it the same as ours? Is it better? How about kids in other cities or other states or other countries? What are the costs for them to have what they have?
- What kind of food is available in our neighborhood? How much fresh food is available? How much packaged? How many grocery stores are there? How many restaurants? Who owns the stores and these other businesses and where do they get their food? How is it different from or the same as what's available in other neighborhoods?
- What are the health issues that most impact our community? Are they at all related to food? How can we find out? Are they different from health issues in other communities? What's the food pyramid? Who designed it? What happens if we get too many or too few or the wrong type of calories in our diets?
- What preservatives or chemicals are in our food? Are there any preservatives allowed in our country that are not allowed in Europe? What are they?

- Where does meat come from? Were the animals treated humanely during their lives? What are the environmental impacts of how they were raised? What are the different grades of meat? What grade is served in our school? Are any of us vegetarians? Why?
- How much of our daily intake of food contains high-fructose corn syrup? How much of our food has corn or corn by-products in it? What about soy? What pesticides are used on these crops and do any of them end up in our food?
- Who makes the laws around food safety? Food labeling? Food production? Do any government officials profit from private food industry?
- What is organic food and how is it different from conventionally grown food? Who has the most access to organic foods? How much does it cost compared to nonorganic food?
- Is access to food related to freedom? Is food an issue of civil or human rights? What rights ought we to have in relation to food?

Greg: The Gangster Life

- What purposes do gangs serve?
- Why do individuals join gangs?
- What role does a gang play in a community?
- Are all purposes bad?
- Are there any suitable alternatives?
- Why are youth attracted to gangs?

Allison and Anthony: Gentrify Me

- What is gentrification and why does it occur in cities?
- What are the positive outcomes of gentrification? What are the negative outcomes?
- What neighborhoods in our city are currently being gentrified?
- Who moves into gentrified neighborhoods? Where do people who lived there before go? What can we do about it?

Angelica: After Food

- What do we eat in the cafeteria? What do we like to eat at home? What food is good for us? Do you think cafeteria food is tasty or healthy? What's the evidence? What's the alternative?
- What foods do you tend to finish? Do you have enough time to eat in school? Do you ever think about the food you're about to throw

away? Do you ever feel sorry for throwing the food away because it's wasteful? Where do you think it goes?

- Do you wish you could take it home with you? How many people do you imagine we could feed with the food we throw away in our lunchroom?
- Does our school recycle? Can we do a survey of how many garbage bags we generate daily, weekly, yearly in our cafeteria alone?

Ben: Check out This Plant!

- Is this plant green?
- Does this plant feel things?
- What does this plant feel? How does this plant feel?
- How do you know?
- What nourishes this plant? What does this plant nourish?
- Does this plant have a purpose? Do we live among plants or do plants live among us?
- How do you know?

Jesse: Music and U:

- Who is your favorite artist?
- What is your favorite music?
- Why do you like it? What does it promote? Where did you first hear it? What do you like about it? Is it relevant to your life?
- Who promotes this music? What's in it for the artist? What's in it for the record company, Wall Street, MTV, VH1? What's in it for you? What's in it for your mom? What's in it for the world?

Eli: Why Are We Here?

- Is school really necessary? Why? Is education an adequate preparation for future living? Should education be representative of the larger life?
- Is education as we practice it part of the process of social progress?
- How do we escape from this place?
- Peace out!

Problem-posing and question-asking is the central strategy of the taboo. This is the stance of challenging convention, questioning common sense, unsettling orthodoxy. This is teaching the taboo.

Coda

... it takes a lot to change the world:
Anger and tenacity. Science and indignation,
the quick initiative, the long reflection,
cold patience and infinite perseverance,
understanding of the particular case, and understanding of the larger whole:
Only the lessons of reality can teach us to transform reality.

—Bertolt Brecht, "Einverständnis"

It may seem, with all the huge forces arrayed against us, that teaching based on empowerment and transformation is quixotic if not downright crazy. In the first place, to be a critical and enlightening teacher-for-freedom demands a deep and constantly renewing commitment to understanding more thoroughly and embracing more fully the students and communities before us. It means exploring as well as the relation of forces in the ongoing struggle.

The Italian Marxist Antonio Gramsci in the 1930s elaborated the ways that "people with power maintain domination over ordinary people through the control of ideas as much as through the exertion or threat of force." Paulo Freire in the 1960s challenged the accepted common sense of his day, arguing that "Ordinary people limit themselves by rejecting ideas that grow from personal experience and instead adopt ideas from the class that rules them." And C.L.R. James, the Caribbean revolutionary, wrote in the 1970s that "the artistic expressions of ordinary people contain truths essential for social change."

Authoritarian forces often control departments of education, universities, legislatures, and school boards, but they are, in spite of their apparent power, the weaker force. After all, their continued exercise of power depends on the acquiescence, the acceptance, of the millions of students and teachers in the schools.

Uneven struggles are everywhere. Take U.S. military adventures over-seas where the military finds itself again and again in impossible-to-win situations, something that happened in Vietnam and that is happening now in Iraq and Afghanistan. U.S. military forces manage to control base areas and to apply huge forces of violence and destruction against a population, but they can never win the war because no one likes occupation and so people resist, learning over time better and better means of resistance. This is now described in the Pentagon as asymmetrical warfare, a confrontation that pits overwhelming military power with massive people power.

In reality, asymmetrical warfare is a familiar theme throughout struggles against invaders and occupiers. Milan Kundera describes the audacity, even euphoria, of Czech citizens in 1968 when they defied the Soviet invasions, sometimes with graffiti, sometimes with shouts and sticks, and sometimes by wantonly kissing one another in front of the tanks. Civil rights activists experienced a phenomenon they called a "freedom high," in which demonstrators who had been set upon felt delighted, expansive, all-powerful even as they were being hauled away to jail, because they realized that this is all the enemy can do to us, this is all they've got, and it's not enough. They had to warn one another against making tactical mistakes, showing too much bravado under the adrenaline of a freedom high. Examples go on and on. Incredible bravery, growing knowledge in tactics to confront the invader, a shifting of the initiative.

In schooling, too, we have an asymmetrical struggle. On one side sit the well-funded and certified experts in their semi-feudal, ultra-hierarchical, hyper-competitive institutions. On all the other sides are the warm and trembling lives of real people, their hopes and dreams, their humor and desire for pleasure, their tendency toward mutual aid and cooperation. The powerful seek to impose their will by ever greater repression, the regime of test and punish. But somehow, with all their guns, all their power, they are the weak ones. There is a kind of euphoria in confronting the highly armed but ultimately powerless enemy. In spite of their resources and in spite of their fire power, they fail to make inroads with the millions of students.

Teachers who teach the taboo defy power and essentially switch allegiances: They move from being petty officers in the campaign of control and reproduction to becoming cultural guerrillas on the side of the irregulars, the students, parents, and communities. Not only are those who hold the purse strings and the power isolated, but, inevitably, they are not going to be able to win. We need the confidence, the audacity, to understand how we can do the work that must be done on the side of the youth, and how democratic forces can ultimately prevail.

§

To teach the taboo is to invent a pedagogy of insurgency—filled with hopes and dreams, it is sometimes defiant and rude, sometimes subversive, always revolutionary. Its purpose is to awaken whoever is asleep, to stir up whatever is musty or cobwebbed or petrifying. It is a pedagogy for teachers who want to shake up the settled, blow away the fog, and sweep away the dust. Teaching the taboo is picking up an axe in order to break through the heavy layers of ice in which our minds and our spirits have been entombed. Teaching the taboo—heart over heartlessness, mind over mindlessness, enlightenment and liberation over ignorance and entrapment—offers an invitation into a pedagogy of fire for a frozen world.

A pedagogy of the taboo is rooted in the idea that each of us is a work-in-progress—in motion, unruly, growing, stretching, developing, changing, learning—alive and making-meaning and acting in the swirl of a vibrant and dynamic history. This means that we are not living at some imagined point of arrival, all of the past leading inexorably and inevitably to this exact moment, even if all the powerful voices insist that that's the case. It means that this moment is as much an historic moment as any other, as any that's come before, and that we are—individually, collectively—the creators of history. What we do, or fail to do, has significance, and consequences. Another world is not only possible; another world is inevitable. History is unfinished, democracy is largely untried, life is uncertain and unfolding, and so we search for something more, for the rest of our humanity.

The basic questions for teaching the taboo are these:

- Who are we?
- How did we get here?
- Where are we going?
- Why?
- How will we get there?

These questions underline all learning, and there are others that help keep our wobbly inquiry, if not exactly on track, perhaps at least lurching forward:

- How do we know what we know?
- What's the evidence, and where else might we look?
- What is invisible, erased, missing, or denied?
- What is the conventional interpretation? What are alternative possibilities?

- What have we experienced or observed first-hand?
- Whose voice is heard, whose perspective and viewpoint represented?
- Whose interests are served?
- Where is the unnecessary suffering, the unjust hurt?
- Why does any of it matter?

A pedagogy of the taboo is a pedagogy of *curiosity*. It asks us to be inquisitive and brave. It insists that wherever we've come to and whatever the established order of things, we always want to ask the next question.

A pedagogy of the taboo is a pedagogy of the *unknown*. It acknowledges that in an infinite and expanding universe, each of us is finite and limited. What we experience and know is puny, a speck on a dot, infinitesimal. We can always discover more, learn more, know more, and still we can never get to the bottom of it; we can never know all there is to know. We call ourselves works-in-progress, artists-in-residence (and our residency is wherever we happen to be). We search for the banned and the excluded, the segregated and suppressed. We are determined to search for the rest of the story, just as we are destined to fall short.

A pedagogy of the taboo is a pedagogy of *skepticism*. We fashion ourselves happy agnostics, uncynical nonconformists, doubting all the triumphalist master-narratives, all the puffed-up verities and certainties, all the dogma and received wisdom. We accept that we live in a perspectival world, and that diversity just is. We are in search of a kaleidoscope of representations, of meanings, of points of view.

Curiosity and skepticism—these are the markers of the pedagogy of the taboo.

We embrace these qualities and take as our symbol and metaphor the image of the urban dumpster-diver leaping into the wreckage in a joyous, spontaneous, and sustained archaeological dig, searching in the dark, damp recesses toward a truer understanding of life in its infinite possibilities. We become guerrilla teachers in our own college of complexes, intent on agitating, educating, emancipating, provoking, exciting, scandalizing, offending, inspiring, tickling, encouraging.

There is, in fact, no promised land in teaching (or in this life); there is instead that aching persistent tension between reality and possibility. What are we teaching for? We want to stand against ignorance and oppression and subjugation, for example, and against exploitation, unfairness, and unkindness. We want to work toward freedom, for enlightenment and awareness, wide-awakeness, protection of the weak, cooperation, generosity, compassion, and love.

We strive, as Tom Mitchell wrote, for

> complexity without mystification, dialectics without the disabling equivocation of ambivalence . . . recognition of the baffling limits of human knowledge without obscurantism or quietism; and a recognition of the situatedness and contingency of every utterance without a surrender to relativism and without a sacrifice of abiding principles.

Difficult enough, and we also stand in opposition to

> the tendency to obfuscation and mystification; the cult of expertise, whether in academic jargon or the prattlings of policy wonks; the counter cult of false transparency in the oversimplified sound bites of the punditocracy; the simplistic binarisms . . . ; and the reductionism of mass media "information." All of this requires an agile, improvisational sense of balance coupled with a dogged and tireless preparation for the next moment of struggle.[62]

"Insane generosity," Albert Camus writes in *The Rebel*, "is the generosity of rebellion." It may be that man is mortal, he said, "but let us die resisting; and if our lot is complete annihilation, let us not behave in such a way that it seems justice!" Camus speaks of a generosity that consistently refuses injustice, that is determined to allow nothing to pass, and that makes no calculations as to what it offers. "Real generosity toward the future," Camus concludes, "lies in giving all to the present." Giving it all, here and now, the only time we've got.

"I can't do everything," we hear ourselves lamenting. Okay. Can we do anything?

Turn out the lights in this room. . . . Light a candle anywhere and it will challenge the darkness everywhere. One candle. We may not be able to do everything, but we can do something, and something is where we begin.

What we can hope for:

- A sense that injustice can be opposed; that justice can be aspired to
- A sense of ongoing unease
- A spirit of connectedness, of solidarity
- A spirit of outrage tempered by a spirit of generosity
- An open-ended dialogue, the questions always open to debate.
- A full and passionate embrace of the life we're given combined with an eagerness to oppose suffering and injustice is what we have to work with: trudging toward freedom; teaching the taboo.

Endnotes

1. Carini, 1997.
2. Lorde, 1995.
3. Cobb, 2008.
4. See Ransby, 2003.
5. Quotes in this section come from Cobb, 1963.
6. Ibid..
7. Herndon, 1968.
8. Lapham, 2004, p. 104.
9. Kozol, 1992.
10. Haberman, 1991.
11. Kliebard, 2004, p. 170.
12. Rugg, 1941
13. Quoted in Kliebard, 2004, p. 173.
14. Postman, 1971, p. 21.
15. Illich, 1971, p. 3–4
16. Stephens, 1996.
17. Foucault, 1977, p. 223
18. Ibid., p. 197.
19. Ibid., p. 201.
20. Ibid., p. 211.
21. Ibid., p. 228.
22. Ibid., p. 198.
23. Fountain, 2006, p. WK14.
24. Ibid., p. WK14.
25. Foucault, 1977, p. 200.
26. Freire, 1970, p. 81.
27. Conrad, 1901, p. 57.
28. Pratt, 1973, p. 260.
29. Quoted in Watkins, 2001, p. 49.
30. Sale, 1991.
31. Morrison, 1992.
32. Ibid., p. 57.
33. Retamar, 1989.
34. Cesaire, 2002.
35. Quoted in Lee, 2007, p. 178.
36. Quoted in Cole, 2010.
37. Dyson, 2006, pp. 4–5.
38. Ibid., pp. 15–17.
39. Allen, 2008, np.
40. Spiegelman & Sendak, 1993.
41. Hurston, 1928.
42. Giovanni, 1968.
43. Rofes, 2005.
44. Said, 1984.
45. Daley, 2001, np.
46. MacKenzie, 1916.
47. "Debate Military Training: School Pupils Give Views at Panel in Times Hall," 1945.
48. Lipman, 2003.
49. Thomas & Wingert, 2010.
50. Ripley, 2008.
51. Brill, 2009.
52. See Perry, Moses, Wynne, Cortés, & Delpit, 2010.
53. Soep & Chávez, 2010.
54. Lee, 2007.
55. Hoffman, 2007.
56. Cadava, 1997, p. 113
57. Thoreau, 1964, p. 243.
58. Rodriguez, 1983.
59. Derrida, 1998, p. 5.
60. Bourdieu, 1991, p. 45.
61. Derrida, 1998, p. 58.
62. Mitchell, 2005, p. 101.

References

Allen, K. (2008, October 27). Science and the personal. Retrieved June 21, 2010, from http://kimallen.sheepdogdesign.net/cinnamon/

Benson, H. (2005, March 29). Interview with Adrienne Rich. *San Francisco Chronicle.* Available at http://articles.sfgate.com/2005-03-29/entertainment/17363947 _1_poem-merwin-national-book-critics-circle

Bourdieu, P. (1991). *Language and symbolic power.* Cambridge, MA: Harvard University Press.

Brecht, B. (1970). Einverständnis. From The Baden-Baden Lesson on Consent in *The Drama Review.* (Original work published 1929)

Brill, S. (2009, August 31). The rubber room: The battle over New York's worst teachers. *New Yorker.* Retrieved August 4, 2010, from www.newyorker.com/ reporting/2009/08/31/090831fa_fact_brill

Cadava, E. (1997). *Emerson and the climates of history.* Palo Alto, CA: Stanford University Press.

Carini, P. (1997). Foreword. In L. Weber & B. Alberty, *Looking Back and Thinking Forward: Reexaminations of Teaching and Schooling.* New York: Teachers College Press.

Cesaire, A. (2002). "A tempest" (R. Miller, trans.). New York: Theatre Communications Group. (Original work published 1969)

Cobb, C. (1963). Prospectus for a Summer Freedom School Program in Mississippi. In SNCC, *The Student Nonviolent Coordinating Committee Papers, 1959–1972* (Reel 39, File 165, Page 75). Sanford, NC: Microfilming Corporation of America, 1982. Retrieved August 3, 2010, from www.educationanddemocracy.org/ FSCfiles/B_05_ProspForFSchools.htm

Cobb, C. (2008). Organizing freedom schools. In C. M. Payne & C. S. Strickland (Eds.), *Teach Freedom: Education for Liberation in the African-American Tradition.* New York: Teachers College Press.

Cole, K. C. (2010). *Something incredibly wonderful happens: Frank Oppenheimer and the world he made up.* New York: Houghton Mifflin Harcourt.

Conrad, J. (1901). *Heart of darkness.* London: Thomas Nelson and Sons.

Daley, R. (2001). Correspondence: Military academies; Do teachers matter? *Education Next.* Retrieved on August 4, 2010, from www.hoover.org/ publications/ednext/3384806.html

"Debate Military Training: School Pupils Give Views at Panel in Times Hall." (1945, January 20). *New York Times.* Available online at www.nytimes.com/

Derrida, J. (1998). *Monolingualism of the other or, the prosthesis of origin.* Palo Alto, CA: Stanford University Press.

Dorfman, A., & Mattelart, A.. (1971). *How to Read Donald Duck: Imperialist Ideology in the Disney Comic.* New York: International General.

Dyson, F. (2006). *The scientist as rebel.* New York: New York Review of Books.

Ellison, R. (1995). *Invisible man.* New York: Random House. (Original work published 1952)

Foucault, M. (1977). *Discipline and punish: The birth of the prison* (Alan Sheridan, trs.). New York: Vintage Books.

Fountain, H. (2006, April 23). The camera never blinks, but it multiplies. *New York Times,* p. WK14.

Freire, P. (1970). *Pedogogy of the oppressed,* p. 81. New York: Continuum.

Freire, P. (1998). *Teachers as cultural workers: Letters to those who dare to teach.* Boulder, CO: Westview.

Giovanni, N. (1968). Nikki-Rosa. In *Black feeling, Black talk, Black judgment.* New York: HarperCollins.

Haberman, M. (1991). The Pedagogy of Poverty Versus Good Teaching. *Phi Delta Kappan, 73*(4), pp. 290–294.

Herndon, J. (1968). *The Way It Spozed To Be.* New Cork: Boynton/Cook.

Hoffman, M. (2007). *You won't remember me: The schoolboys of Barbiana speak to today.* New York: Teachers College Press.

Hurston, Z. N. (1928, May). How it feels to be colored me. *The World Tomorrow.*

Illich, I. (1971). The breakdown of schools: A problem or a symptom? *Interchange, 2*(4), 1–10.

Kliebard, H. M. (2004). *The struggle for the American curriculum, 1893–1958.* New York: Routledge Falmer.

Kozol, J. (1992). *Savage Inequalities: Children in America's Schools.* New Cork: Crown.

Lapham, L. H. (2004). *Gag Rule: On the Suppression of Dissent and the Stifling of Democracy.* New York: Penguin.

Lee, C. (2007). *Culture, literacy and learning: Taking bloom in the midst of the whirlwind.* New York: Teachers College Press.

Lipman, P. (2003). *High stakes education: Inequality, globalization, and urban school reform.* New York: Routledge.

Lorde, A. (1995). A Litany for Survival. In *Black Unicorn* (p. 31). New York: W. W. Norton.

MacKenzie, J. (1916, September 10). Can schools give military training? *New York Times.* Retrieved August 4, 2010, from http://query.www.nytimes.com/gst/abstract.html?res=9E07E1DD1F31E733A05753C1A96F9C946796D6CF

Makoni, S. (2003). *Black linguistics: Language, society, and politics in Africa and the Americas.* London and New York: Routledge.

Mitchell, W. J. T. (2005). Secular divination: Edward Said's humanism. In H. Bhabha & W. J. T. Mitchell (Eds.), *Edward Said: Continuing the conversation* (pp. 98-108). Chicago: University of Chicago Press.

Morrison, T. (1992). *Playing in the dark: Whiteness and the literary imagination.* Cambridge, MA: Harvard University Press.

Perry, T., & Delpit, L. (1998). *The real Ebonics debate.* New York: Beacon.

Perry, T., Moses, R., Wynne, J., Cortés, E., & Delpit, L. (2010). *Quality education as a constitutional right.* Boston: Beacon.

Postman, N. (1971). *Teaching as a subversive activity.* New York: Delta Books.

Pratt, R. H. (1973). Official report of the Nineteenth Annual Conference of Charities and Correction. In *Americanizing the American Indians: Writings by the "Friends of the Indian" 1880–1900.* Cambridge, MA: Harvard University Press. (Original work published 1892)

Ransby, B. (2003). *Ella Baker and the Black Freedom Movement.* Chapel Hill: University of North Carolina Press.

Retamar, R. F. (1989). *Caliban and other essays.* Minneapolis: University of Minnesota Press.

Ripley, A. (2008, November 26). Rhee tackles classroom challenge. *Time.* Retrieved August 4, 2010, from www.time.com/time/magazine/article/0,9171,1862444,00.html

Rodriguez, R. (1983). *Hunger of Memory.* New York: Bantam.

Rofes, E. (2005). *A radical rethinking of sexuality and schooling: Status quo or status queer.* New York: Rowman and Littlefield.

Rugg, H. (1941). *Man and His Changing Society* (6 vols.). New York: Doubleday.

Russell, B. (1954). *Human society in ethics and politics.* London: Unwin Hyman.

Said, E. (1984). Permission to narrate. In *The London Review of Books* 6(3), 13–17.

Sale, K. (1991). *The Conquest of Paradise: Christopher Columbus and the Columbian Legacy.* New York: Plume.

Soep, E., & Chávez, V. (2010). *Drop that knowledge.* Berkeley: University of California Press.

Spiegelman, A., & Sendak, M. (1993, September 27). In the dumps. *The New Yorker,* p. 80.

Stephens, R. (1996). The art of safe school planning: 40 ways to manage and control student disruptions. *School Administrator, 53*(2), 14–21.

Thomas, E., & Wingert, P. (2010, March 15). Why we must fire bad teachers. *Newsweek.*

Thoreau, H. D. (1964). The last days of John Brown. In C. Bode, (Ed.), *The Portable Thoreau* (p. 243). New York: Penguin. (Original work published 1860)

Watkins, W. (2001). *The White architects of Black education.* New York: Teachers College Press.

West, C. (1992). Prisoner of hope. Quoted in Anna Deavere Smith's *Twilight, L.A.,* Public Broadcasting Service.

Woodson, C. G. (1972). *The mis-education of the Negro.* New York: AMS Press. (Original work published 1933)

Zamora, D. (1994). *Life for each.* London: Katabasis.

About the Authors

Rick Ayers is a university instructor and founder of the Communication Arts and Sciences small school at Berkeley High School, and teaches at the University of San Francisco.

William Ayers is a school reform activist and a Distinguished Professor of Education and Senior University Scholar at the University of Illinois at Chicago.